Better Homes and Gardens®

step-by-step

perennials

Patricia Taylor

Better Homes and Gardens® Books
Des Moines, Iowa

Better Homes and Gardens® Books
An imprint of Meredith® Books

Step-by-Step Perennials
Senior Editor: Marsha Jahns
Production Manager: Douglas Johnston

Vice President and Editorial Director: Elizabeth P. Rice
Executive Editor: Kay Sanders
Art Director: Ernest Shelton
Managing Editor: Christopher Cavanaugh

President, Book Group: Joseph J. Ward
Vice President, Retail Marketing: Jamie L. Martin
Vice President, Direct Marketing: Timothy Jarrell

Meredith Corporation
Chairman of the Executive Committee: E. T. Meredith III
Chairman of the Board and Chief Executive Officer:
    Jack D. Rehm
President and Chief Operating Officer: William T. Kerr

Produced by ROUNDTABLE PRESS, INC.
Directors: Susan E. Meyer, Marsha Melnick
Executive Editor: Amy T. Jonak
Editorial Director: Anne Halpin
Senior Editor: Jane Mintzer Hoffman
Design: Brian Sisco, Susan Evans, Sisco & Evans, New York
Photo Editor: Marisa Bulzone
Assistant Photo Editor: Carol Sattler
Encyclopedia Editor: Henry W. Art and Storey
    Communications, Inc., Pownal, Vermont
Horticultural Consultant: Christine M. Douglas
Copy Editors: Paula Bakule, Sue Heinemann, Amy K. Hughes
Proofreader: Cathy Peck
Editorial Assistant: Alexis Wilson
Step-by-Step Photography: Derek Fell
Garden Plans: Elayne Sears and Storey Communications, Inc.

All of us at Meredith® Books are dedicated to providing you
with the information and ideas you need for successful gardening. We guarantee your satisfaction with this book for as
long as you own it. If you have any questions, comments, or
suggestions, please write to us at:

Meredith® Books, *Garden Books*
Editorial Department, RW206
1716 Locust St.
Des Moines, IA 50309–3023

STEP-BY-STEP
Perennials

The Perennial Garden

*t*he beauty of a perennial garden is that it offers endless possibilities for colorful flowers, textured foliage, and sophisticated garden designs—year after year. ● Perennial gardens come in many sizes, shapes, and styles, from the exuberant displays of colorful flowers in an American prairie setting to sumptuously formal English borders. ● Behind this wide variety, however, lies a common base: all perennial gardens are composed of beautiful plants that reappear for at least several years. ● Although not every perennial may be suited to your individual garden, the large number of available plants makes the task of creating a perennial garden seem daunting. But starting a garden need not be a chore, and this book will guide you step-by-step along the way. ● The chapters that follow, accompanied by beautiful photographs, show you how to work with these versatile flowers to create a unique garden that is suited to both your lifestyle and your geographic area.

*T*he concept of a perennial garden dates back to ancient times when wealthy Persians began to construct open-air rooms within their homes and fill them with plants. The rooms served as places for retreat, where one could rest and contemplate the beauty of nature. The English word "paradise" comes from the Greek word "paradeisos," meaning "park" or "pleasure ground."

In those days there was no formal distinction between perennials, annuals, bulbs, and shrubs. People chose plants solely for their beauty and their fragrance. As people became aware of the number of available plants, the scientific discipline of botany emerged, and with it the attempt to classify plants. To this day, however, botanists are struggling with how to correctly define and group plants.

In general the term "perennial" describes a plant whose foliage and flowers disappear during winter but whose roots stay alive. After an enforced resting period, the roots send forth new growth and flowers. "Herbaceous" perennials, discussed in this book, have soft, green stems, not woody, brown ones like those on trees and shrubs.

Under this definition plants that store food and energy in underground structures—crocuses and bearded irises, for example—are not true perennials. Rather they are corms or bulbs or tubers. Similarly, plants that come back every year through reseeding, rather than through overwintering—crabgrass and cleomes, for example—are annuals, not perennials.

Then there is that odd group, known as biennials, that seed themselves but do not flower until a year or two later. Since the roots on these plants remain alive throughout the winter, many people think of them as perennials, and you will find several mentioned in this book. Foxglove (*Digitalis*) is one popular example of a biennial that can winter over—pass a winter in dormancy before emerging to bloom in the following spring or summer.

Until the past century or so, gardening was the province of the rich. Although gardening advanced considerably due to the efforts of dedicated horticulturists among the lords and ladies seeking to beautify their estates, gardening also became a status symbol. The wealthier one was, the larger and grander was the garden.

Less affluent folk, such as the early American colonists, also had their garden plots, but these were small areas set aside for utilitarian purposes. These gardens contained the herbs and spices needed for healing and cooking.

Until some time after the American Revolution, annuals and tender perennials were generally absent from ornamental estate gardens both here and overseas because they could not survive the colder northern climates. The invention of sheet glass in 1833, however, made the construction of greenhouses relatively inexpensive, and radically transformed the garden scene.

At the same time, plant explorers were collecting vast numbers of exotic plants from Africa, Australia, and Latin America and shipping them to England and the European continent. Although these annuals could not survive the bitter winters outdoors, they did thrive in the protection of greenhouses.

Gardeners discovered that the plants could be set outside in early spring and would start flowering soon after. Even better, many of these plants, such as marigolds and geraniums, produced all summer long.

In England, the Victorian craze for bedding with annuals set in, and continuous, riotous color in controlled designs soon became the order of the day.

This lovely shade garden provides an oasis of greenery right outside the door. The feathery pink and red plumes of astilbe highlight the ferns and lungwort (Pulmonaria).

Old-fashioned Perennials

The following perennials were all grown in gardens two or more centuries ago, and are still delightful today. All are good candidates for cottage gardens.

Red Valerian
(Centranthus ruber).
Red, pink, or white flowers throughout summer with good-looking grayish blue foliage.

Foxglove
(Digitalis purpurea).
Spires of pink to white flowers. Once a staple of medieval herb gardens. Source of the heart drug digitalis.

Tawny Daylily
(Hemerocallis fulva 'Kwanso').
The common orange roadside flower. Sturdy and easy to grow in all types of soil.

Dame's Rocket
(Hesperis matronalis).
Fragrant perennial covered for a long period with lavender or white flowers. Naturalized at edges of wooded areas.

Evergreen Candy-tuft
(Iberis sempervirens).
Sparkling white flowers in spring. Tidy and low growing, with dark green, needlelike leaves.

Rose Campion
(Lychnis coronaria).
Felty-gray foliage and brilliant magenta flowers. Grown in this country before the American Revolution.

Beebalm
(Mondarda didyma).
Red flowers attract hummingbirds. Pink, white, and purple cultivars also handsome in garden and arrangements. Native plant used as tea substitute during Revolution.

Feverfew
(Tanacetum parthenium, *also known as* Chrysanthemum parthenium).
White, daisylike flowers all summer through light frosts. Brought to the United States by early settlers.

Almost anyone could grow perennial flowers at this point, but only a select few had the wealth to build greenhouses, hire gardeners to manage them, and obtain the seed for the new plants.

In this country, Americans followed the British gardening dogma. If the British decreed that annual beds were the height of fashion, then American gardeners of all income levels followed suit. Leading American landscape architects such as Andrew Jackson Dowling in the mid-1800s and Jens Jensen at the turn of this century pleaded with Americans to incorporate low-maintenance perennials, particularly those native to the United States, in their gardens. Nonetheless annuals remained the rage.

Only when the British began to use perennials did American gardeners follow suit. Two Englishwomen in particular inspired the change in Americans' opinions of perennials: Gertrude Jekyll and Vita Sackville-West. Jekyll, who came to the fore in the late 1800s and early 1900s, championed the beauty of perennial flowers and their importance in landscape design. Her gardens contained sweeping borders that were subtly orchestrated compositions of color, form, and texture. From the 1930s until her death in 1962, Vita Sackville-West designed her gardens at Sissinghurst castle in Kent, England, with perennials incorporated into a series of smaller "rooms" or theme gardens. In the United States, Henry Francis du Pont was one of the first Americans to copy the new English fondness for perennials. From the early- to mid-1900s, du Pont created the sumptuous gardens at Winterthur, his estate in Delaware—using almost exclusively perennial plants.

Interest in any type of ornamental gardening, both in the United States and abroad, dwindled with the outbreak of World War II. The postwar housing boom of the 1950s rekindled interest in gardening as Americans began to search for ways to decorate the bare landscapes surrounding tract homes that had been constructed on former farm fields or wastelands. Annuals remained popular until the 1970s, when once again, Americans looked to England and saw beautiful creations. Americans began to create manageable-sized gardens crammed with perennials. There were stately blue delphiniums, towering foxgloves, pastel aubrietas, and many other garden gems—all perennials Americans saw in photos of the great English estate gardens. In all but a few select places, English-style gardens died; not because of poor care, but because of the different climate.

Slowly but surely, Americans discovered a wealth of perennial flowers that flourished right in their own climates. As a result, a very individualistic, American style of gardening has begun to emerge. Agaves, aloes, and sedums, for example, add sculptured grace to dry western gardens while peonies, clove pinks (Dianthus), August lilies (Hosta plantaginea), and sweet autumn clematis (C. maximowicziana) create lush, fragrant settings in the Northeast.

This regional approach to gardening style promotes ease of care, as plants' cultural needs are matched to available growing conditions.

The pleasures of perennials are particularly apparent as the seasons change. A perennial garden, unlike one bedded out solely with annuals, is ever-changing. There are perennials for spring, summer, and fall. All can be combined in one garden setting, creating changing color schemes throughout the garden year and—when the flowers fade—leaving behind interesting textural and foliage combinations.

Sunny coreopsis, a summer favorite, is especially well suited to informal gardens. In this border it blooms after bearded iris, whose sword-like foliage can be seen in the background.

CHAPTER 1

Designing Your Perennial Garden

given the wide variety of fragrant, colorful flower combinations available, developing a design for your perennial garden can be an exciting adventure. • Begin with the premise that your perennial garden will suit your tastes only and will be as small or as grand as you please. Remember, there is no "right" plant combination or "wrong" blooming sequence. Beauty is in the eye of the creator, especially with perennial gardens. • Your options, however, are not entirely unlimited. Geographical location and local site conditions both play a large part in design choices. You can't, for example, have an English cottage garden in an arid Southwest setting or a prairie garden in a heavily wooded lot. • This chapter will show you how to work around the constraints of climate, soil type, and light and how to take advantage of the many beautiful opportunities available to you as you construct your perennial garden.

Best Site

Most people plant an ornamental garden where they can best look at it. After all, what is the sense of having beautiful perennial flowers if you rarely see them? In deciding upon a location, first choose a spot for your garden that will let you enjoy its view most often. Your view of the garden can be from any of a number of places, such as the view from your kitchen window or from the walk leading to your front door. After you realize how easy it is to grow perennials, you may want to expand your beds or start new ones on other areas of your property. But place your first perennial bed where you'll receive the greatest and most immediate pleasure from your garden.

Once you've selected a spot, examine the possible constraints this location may present, such as geological, climatic, or other factors that may make this selection less than ideal. Is the proposed garden area excessively rocky? Do heavy rains leave a small pond in your yard that lasts for as long as a full day? Will children be playing ball nearby?

Give yourself time to evaluate any problems you can anticipate. If you have chosen a garden spot on a sunny, school-day morning, for example, you might change your mind after looking at the site following a heavy rain on a Saturday when the kids are running around. While errant soccer balls or poor drainage don't present impossible obstacles, they do make it more difficult to maintain the garden. If you're averse to such extra work, look around for another growing spot that demands less effort. If you have a choice, select a site that has relatively level ground, good drainage, reasonably rich soil, protection from strong winds, and some sun.

Perennials bordering the path to the front door add color to an otherwise plain lawn and offer a gracious welcome to visitors. The pink, blue, and white color scheme complements the blue-gray color of the house.

Many perennials love the sun. Some of the standouts in this sunny pink-and-gold border are a pink cultivar of Achillea, yellow daisylike Anthemis, *and purple loosestrife* (Lythrum), *which may become invasive in wet soil.*

A perennial garden can thrive in a shady spot if you choose the right plants. In this spring garden, carpets of blue lungworts (Pulmonaria angustifolia) *and red-violet primroses* (Primula 'Wanda') *cover the ground.*

A garden on a slope adds color, prevents soil from eroding, and eliminates the difficult job of mowing grass. Cranesbills (Geranium), *lady's-mantle* (Alchemilla), *irises, and peonies bloom in this sunny garden.*

Beds and Borders

Gardens come in all sizes and shapes. Those that are free-standing, such as an oval planting in the middle of a grassy slope, are known as beds. Those that abut structures, such as buildings or fences, or skirt the edges of yards or walkways are known as borders.

The design of a garden bed—as opposed to a border—is open-ended because you create the boundaries and determine the shape. In ages past, beds were usually symmetrical and consisted of carefully placed rectangles filled with aromatic plants, such as herbs and roses. The English romantic era of gardening, launched in the 1700s, rejected such precision in favor of more naturalistic settings. Beds became random, irregular shapes that followed the contour of the property rather than preconceived geometrical layouts.

Designing a formal garden bed is rather easy because you only have to lay out geometrical figures such as squares, triangles, or ovals and then fill them in with plants. To be really grand, like the French

1 *When laying out a new bed or border, use lengths of hose to outline the shape of the garden. Adjust the hose to get the size and shape you want before you start to dig.*

Gardens come in many shapes and sizes. Here, masses of aloes and agaves appear to march down a slope.

The curved path through this garden, defined by the edges of the adjacent beds, softens the formality of neatly sheared hedges and shrubs.

A round island bed adds a bounty of color to an expanse of manicured lawn. Repeating some plants in nearby borders adds a feeling of continuity to this garden.

A stone path winds though romantic drifts of flowers. In the foreground are blue delphiniums and a silvery artemisia (Artemisia arborescens).

Rectangular borders, such as this colorful array of flowers, are ideal in front of a fence, hedge, or wall.

2 *Next outline the perimeter of the garden by digging with a sharp spade along the inside of the hose. At this point, you can remove the hose if you wish.*

3 *To remove the sod, cut vertically around a patch of turf, then push the spade horizontally under the sod to loosen it. Lift the sod away from the soil.*

4 *Repeat the procedure until the surface of the garden is clear. Stack the sod in layers, grass to grass then soil to soil, and let it decompose into compost.*

landscaper André Le Nôtre who designed the gardens at Versailles, you can create elaborate patterns with the forms of the beds.

Designing an informal bed is a bit trickier. You have to figure out how much curve and undulation you want. The best method for deciding the shape of your garden is to arrange garden hoses along the proposed lines. Step back and look at the design. If one part sticks out too much, shorten the curve or perhaps lengthen another section of the garden. Remember, it's a lot easier to move around a hose than to dig an outline and then cover it up and start all over again.

Whether formal or informal, the open nature of a garden bed dictates that it can be seen from all sides. When you construct this kind of garden, you have to give a great deal of thought to the placement of plants.

Borders are somewhat easier to create because you can work around a structure or boundary that already exists. As with garden beds, borders can be either formal or informal. Often the backdrop—a round gazebo or a right angle of a house corner—will influence your choice of a straight or a curved edge to your border. If you opt for a curved, informal edge, haul out your hoses again and use them to determine the shape you want.

There is much debate as to the proper front-to-back depth of a border. Current garden design fashion holds that it should equal twice the height of the tallest plant. This equation leads to rather deep borders, given that a medium-sized perennial is 3 to 4 feet tall and a giant perennial easily tops 6 feet.

Whenever your border is more than 5 feet deep, you will have to plan for access to the plants that are farthest from the front. You can reach these plants from a narrow, almost hidden walk behind the border or from a stone path that winds through the middle of the border.

Formal vs. Informal

A formal garden has defined boundaries and carefully placed plants arranged in straight lines. The controlling hand of the gardener is quite evident in a formal garden design. An informal garden appears to wander about at will. It is filled with curves and soft shapes and appears to have plants that burst all bounds. Critics might say that the former style is prissy and the latter is messy, but in fact, most gardens incorporate a bit of both.

Formal gardens appeal to those who like a neater appearance. Each perennial is assigned a specific space and growth spread, so these gardens do not contain invasive plants. Ideally, flowers that need to be constantly deadheaded to remove their faded blossoms, such as Stokes' asters *(Stokesia laevis)*, are also banned from such pristine gardens.

Autumn Joy sedum, a plant that does not spread or self-sow, is a perfect perennial for a formal garden. It has long-season interest with blue-green, succulent foliage, flower buds that begin to appear in midsummer, and then a great end-of-season show with pink flowers slowly aging to coppery bronze and then wine red. Elegant lilies and delphiniums, carefully staked of course, are also a natural addition to a formal garden.

In contrast to the neatness and elegance of a formal garden, informal beds are exuberant. They tend to have rippled borders and drifts of flower color that run through planting schemes. And while purists may argue that flowers should be deadheaded in an informal setting, there is more room for laxity in maintenance here than in a formal garden.

There is a fine line between informal and messy, however, and if not maintained, an informal border can become an unattractive hodgepodge of flowers roaming at will. Charming plants such as mallow (*Malva alcea* 'Fastigiata') self-seed with abandon, so unwanted seedlings must be weeded out. The reliable black-eyed Susan (*Rudbeckia fulgida*) spreads at a steady pace and needs to be pulled back periodically to be kept in bounds.

If you opt for the beguiling charms of an informal border, choose restrained plants, such as balloon flowers *(Platycodon grandiflorus)*, hostas, hellebores, and butterfly weeds *(Asclepias tuberosa)*. Don't plant the flowers in a tight, straight line; group them in casual "drifts," so they look natural. Then add one or two gadabouts, such as cheery yellow sundrops *(Oenothera fruticosa)* or summer-blue, perennial cornflowers *(Centaurea montana)*, and carefully monitor their activities.

Well-maintained plants in geometrically shaped beds with neatly clipped hedges and shrubs typify formal gardens.

Informal gardens feature exuberant plants in flowing, soft-edged drifts.

Uncommon Perennials

Unusual plants are a welcome addition to any perennial garden. Here are several to try.

Pheasant's-Eye
(Adonis amurensis).
A late winter woodland gem with bright yellow flowers and fernlike foliage.

Hardy Begonia
(Begonia grandis).
Red undercoated leaves closely resemble those of the house-plant angel-wing begonia (Begonia coccinea). *Lovely pink flowers in early fall.*

Yellow Corydalis
(Corydalis lutea).
Tiny, bright yellow flowers nestle among elegant, blue-green foliage late spring to fall.

Small's Beard-Tongue
(Penstemon Smallii).
Charming pink and white flowers in early summer.

False Solomon's-Seal
(Smilacina racemosa).
Handsome native plant with graceful, arching foliage and clusters of white flowers in spring.

Working with Plant Heights

*D*esigning with perennials is fun because there are no hard-and-fast rules. Just when you read that tall plants go in the back of the garden and short ones up front, a garden designer will come along and dispute this theory.

A large, bold plant, for example, such as the towering, felty-gray mullein *(Verbascum bombyciferum)* looks great placed up front at the extreme side of a border so its grandeur will not in any way be masked by other plants. Short, spring-flowering perennials such as Virginia bluebells *(Mertensia virginica)* can easily be situated in the back of the border where their

sky-blue blossoms will flourish before the emergence of taller, later-blooming plants.

Other designers say that tall, slim, spiky flowers such as lobelias and delphiniums look dramatic in the middle of a border. Because they are slender, they do not fully block out the plants behind them.

Nonetheless, the tried-and-true practice of grouping plants by height is the best rule to follow when you first plan a perennial garden. As you become more familiar with plants and wish to experiment with new ideas, you can then try moving plants around for different looks.

Siberian bugloss (Brunnera macrophylla) *has sky-blue flowers floating on delicate stems above a low clump of leaves.*

Soapwort (Saponaria officinalis) *is low-growing, with mats of leaves and trailing stems.*

*Catmint (*Nepeta 'Six Hills Giant'*) is a medium-sized plant that forms loose, vigorous clumps. Like most other mints, it spreads.*

Dull as it may sound, by placing a row of short plants in front of a row of medium-sized plants in front of a row of tall plants, you can create a border that is quite varied and dramatic when the width and forms of different perennials are taken into account.

Two old-fashioned plants illustrate this point nicely. Many types of plantain lily (*Hosta* species) have foliage clumps that easily stretch to 3 feet, while the more restrained wild bleeding-heart *(Dicentra eximia)* rarely reaches 1 foot in width. Though both are approximately the same height and best placed in the front of the border, the difference in width offers a lively contrast.

Width differences can become even more dramatic in the back of a border. There, large plants such as boltonia *(B. asteroides)* spread out over 4 feet while stately but slim perennials such as 5-foot-tall New England asters *(A. novae-angliae)* rarely exceed 18 inches in width.

False dragonhead (Physostegia virginiana) *has slender spires of flowers in pink, white, or lilac.*

Coralbells (Heuchera 'Old La Rochette') *has charming, light-pink flowers on tall, slender stems.*

Black snakeroot (Cimicifuga racemosa) *is an excellent background plant, growing up to 8 feet tall.*

Textures

*A*ll plants have a textural form, made up of unique foliage and flower characteristics. Consider each plant's total appearance—whether it's bold and sculptural, small and bushy, or lacy and airy—when deciding what to plant in your perennial garden. The combinations and permutations of different textures are almost endless, and they present a wonderful challenge to designing a garden. Think of working with texture as a way of furnishing your garden with contrasting shapes and forms. Carefully chosen combinations of plant and leaf textures make gardens interesting when flowers are not in bloom.

Some plants are so striking that they exude a certain feeling or texture. Baby's breath *(Gypsophila paniculata)*, for example, is covered with masses of tiny white flowers that seem to twinkle in the air. This plant has an airy nature and needs a solid backing, such as an evergreen hedge, to set it off.

Bold plants, such as rodgersia *(R. pinnata)* with its large, compound, deep green leaves and clusters of small white flowers, can stand on their own and need to be carefully placed so that they serve as a dramatic focal point but do not overwhelm the garden.

Small, delicate plants such as the maidenhair fern *(Adiantum* species), with its delicate foliage made up of fan-shaped leaflets, would be lost as individual specimens when placed next to the bolder rodgersia. A large grouping of these ferns would be needed to counterbalance the overall stronger texture of the rodgersia. For an entirely different combination of textures, the ferns could be planted next to lady's-mantle *(Alchemilla mollis)*, also a short plant but with

This artful combination marries the prickly texture of globe thistle (Echinops ritro) *with the prominent cone-shaped centers of purple coneflowers* (Echinacea purpurea).

Bergenia cordifolia *has bold, sculptural leaves that spread close to the ground: arising from them are abundant clusters of rich pink, tubular flowers.*

rounded, scalloped foliage that serves as a pleasing contrast to the delicate leaves of the ferns.

In addition to choosing plants with complementary overall textures, select plants with interesting combinations of foliage textures. Different hostas, for example, can be the same size and have similarly shaped leaves and yet exhibit dramatically different textures. Their leaves can be puckered ('Bright Lights'), glossy ('Royal Standard'), smooth and velvety ('Moon Glow'), or undulating ('Ground Master'). The contrasts in foliage texture among these different plants will provide a pleasing design pattern.

Other plants, such as many artemisias, have feathery textures that do not contrast significantly enough to plant in a pleasing group. Placing the low-growing 'Silver Mound' artemisia next to the taller

A variety of leaf textures, clockwise from top left: swordlike Iris *foliage, softly fuzzy lamb's-ears* (Stachys), *scalloped and crinkled lady's-mantle* (Alchemilla), *smooth stonecrop* (Sedum), *and feathery artemisia.*

'Powis Castle' artemisia leads to some variation in height but little in texture. A bolder, more solid-leaved plant, such as the furry, gray lamb's-ears *(Stachys byzantina)*, is needed to set off the lightness of the artemisia foliage.

The delicate flowers of Siberian bugloss (Brunnera macrophylla) *provide a textural contrast with the plant's own leaves and the bold foliage of the hosta behind them.*

The soft-textured, airy flower panicles of eulalia grass (Miscanthus sinensis *'Silver Feather'*) *set off the misty lavender blossoms of Russian sage* (Perovskia atriplicifolia).

The Importance of Foliage

*F*oliage is a particularly important factor in designing with perennials because leaves are on view much longer than any flowers. Indeed, some gardeners actually prefer to concentrate on leaf characteristics rather than on flowers. This is not surprising because perennial foliage comes in such colors as purple, cream, yellow, and silver. Often, these colors are splashed or streaked onto a green background and create beautiful patterns.

In sunny gardens, for example, foliage combinations of purple and bright silver are particularly outstanding. One form of the native alumroot (*Heuchera* 'Palace Purple') has rich purple maple-leaf-shaped foliage that lasts throughout summer. When this alumroot is placed next to clumps of the soft, needle-like foliage of 'Silver Mound' artemisia (*A. schmid-tiana* 'Silver Mound'), the result is a beautiful, low-maintenance combination that provides color throughout the growing season—without any flowers.

To light up the dimness of a shade garden, choose plants with gray- or white-speckled foliage. The popular variegated hostas (*Hosta fortunei* cultivars) are a particular favorite. Their leaves are edged with brilliant white and pair beautifully with dark green plants such as Siberian bugloss *(Brunnera macrophylla)* or Jacob's-ladder *(Polemonium caeruleum).*

Lungwort *(Pulmonaria saccharata)* is another shade-garden gem valued more for its striking, long-lasting foliage than for its blue early-spring flowers. Its leaves are sprinkled with gray spots and stand out even in the darkest settings.

Perennials are mostly foliage for a good part of the growing season. In this garden, foliage is the main feature. A gold-edged hosta dominates the foreground. Amsonia tabernaemontana (pale blue flowers) and lady's-mantle (yellow-green flowers) both have attractive leaves when not in bloom. Goatsbeard (Aruncus dioicus) anchors the background.

Heuchera *'Palace Purple' has deep burgundy leaves and delicate sprays of tiny white flowers.*

The spiky leaves of New Zealand flax (Phormium tenax) *come in several colors and striped patterns.*

Hostas offer great versatility. Their foliage may be smooth, quilted, or puckered, lime green to blue-green, and streaked or edged with white, gold, or, like this one, blue.

This interesting duo of low-growing perennials combines fuzzy, silver pussytoes (Antennaria dioica var. rosea) with glossy, burgundy bugleweed (Ajuga reptans 'Bronze Beauty').

Foliage Perennials

Most gardeners think of hostas when they think of foliage plants. Here are some other perennials with eye-catching foliage.

'Silver Mound' Artemisia (A. schmidtiana 'Silver Mound'). Delicate, silvery, needlelike leaves form neat mounds when grown in full sun.

'Royal Red' Heuchera (H. villosa 'Royal Red'). Shade-garden gem has large, maplelike leaves with glossy, dark wine-red coloring.

Variegated Yellow Flag (Iris pseudacorus 'Variegata'). Tall, swordlike leaves edged with creamy-yellow stripes.

White Nancy (Lamium maculatum 'White Nancy'). Low-growing silver leaves edged in green.

Plume Poppy (Macleaya cordata). Perennial giant with huge, deeply lobed green leaves undercoated with grayish, felty texture.

Working with Color

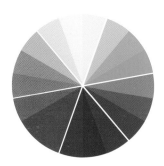

The Color Wheel

A basic understanding of the theory behind the color wheel will help you mix pleasing color combinations in your garden.

*E*xperimenting with color brings out the artist in every gardener. Many gardeners, however, do not wish to place artistic standards on their pleasurable activities. For these people the goal is to have a variety of flowers to admire in their yard or to bring in for arrangements. The loveliness of these flowers can be enhanced with a working knowledge of color theory.

Whether you are a casual gardener who simply wants to grow pretty flowers or an artist who wants to create a living masterpiece, you need to be familiar with the color wheel. At its simplest, the color wheel consists of three primary colors: red, blue, and yellow. When each color blends with its neighbor, intermediary colors are created. Thus, red and blue are the parents of purple; blue and yellow meld to produce green; and yellow and red mix together to create orange. These intermediary colors can also meld with others, resulting in literally hundreds of different colors.

There are several ways to work with such a richness of color choice in your garden.

▼ Plant an assortment of mixed colors and hope for the best. With this "potluck" approach, the plants that survive determine the color scheme.

▼ Work with harmonious colors. These are colors that are closely related to one another on the color wheel. Red, orange, and gold is one example of a harmonious color combination. Flowers in these shades, such as red blackberry lilies *(Belamcanda chinensis)*, orange daylilies *(Hemerocallis fulva)*, and golden yellow swordleaf inula *(I. ensifolia)*, also blend together harmoniously.

▼ Work with contrasting colors. These are colors that are far apart on the color wheel, such as blues and oranges and purples and yellows. To add color contrast to the harmonious perennial scheme described above, substitute the deep blue, stately delphinium for the red blackberry lily.

This brilliantly contrasting color combination plays yellow Achillea taygetea *against magenta* Geranium × 'Ann Folkard'.

▼ Use shades and tints of a single color. Probably the most famous single-color garden is Vita Sackville-West's white garden at Sissinghurst in England. Many other gardeners have tried to copy it, but most soon discover that working with a single color is extremely difficult.

Keep in mind that every color has a wide range of brightness and saturation. Brightness refers to the amount of white or black contained in the color, and saturation refers to the purity of the color. White flowers, for example, can contain touches of gray, blue, pink, yellow, or green. Thus you need to consider how these subtleties blend or contrast. When improperly mixed, the result can be chaotic even though only one color is used.

A softly harmonious garden of columbines (Aquilegia) blends shades of lavender with deep blue-violet, touches of white, and carmine-red accents.

White wands of gooseneck loosestrife (Lysimachia clethroides) add sparkle to a sophisticated pairing of two different shades of orange—salmon astilbe and pumpkin-colored daylilies (Hemerocallis fulva).

Warm and Cool Colors

A knowledge of the theory of warm and cool colors will enable you to visually manipulate the look of your garden. Warm colors, such as red, bright yellow, orange, and creamy white, make the garden seem closer. Cool colors, such as blues or violets, make the boundary or edge of your garden seem farther away. Although pure white is technically a neutral color, a yellow-white such as ivory is considered warm, and a sparkling bluish-white, cool.

Gertrude Jekyll, the renowned turn-of-the-century British garden designer, was one of the preeminent exponents of using these principles in garden design. In many of her gardens, she used cool colors, such as blue, mauve, and quiet silver, at each end of the border. In the center, Jekyll placed warm colors, such as the beebalm's scarlet red. These colors made the border seem much deeper at the center than it actually was. By carefully choosing a color combination, Jekyll was able to make a plain, rectangular shape appear elongated at each end and wider in the middle.

You can also use warm and cool colors to make your garden beds appear larger or smaller. A small oval bed filled with scarlet Maltese cross *(Lychnis chalcedonica)*, golden coreopsis *(C. lanceolata)*, and red-and-yellow sneezeweed *(Helenium autumnale)*, for example, will appear much larger than a similarly sized oval bed planted with light blue bellflower *(Campanula persicifolia)*, pale moonshine yarrow *(Achillea × 'Moonshine')*, and steely blue globe thistle *(Echinops ritro)*.

To make the scale of the first bed fit better with its surroundings, eliminate one of the reds and add a dark violet-blue, such as *Salvia × superba* 'May Night'. To make the latter bed seem larger, heat up its setting by adding a bright white, such as the wedding phlox *(P. maculata* 'Miss Lingard').

Bright orange butterfly weed (Asclepias tuberosa) *is the focus of this warm orange and yellow garden. The color scheme is freshened with white and softened with touches of blue.*

When planning a color scheme, consider the surroundings. Here, white and gold brightens a cool blue and purple garden that might otherwise blend into the dark green background.

Since daylilies are available in a wide range of warm colors, it is possible to create a handsome border that glows in harmonious tones of red, orange, and yellow.

To tone down a hot combination like this mix of black-eyed Susans, plant a lot of green among and around the bright flowers. In the garden, green softens strong colors.

This subtle garden combines spiky purple salvia with fluffy pink astilbe. Touches of golden coreopsis enliven the cool composition.

A mass of pink pincushion flowers is paired with tubular flowers of Penstemon, *catmint (Nepeta),* and the narrow spikes of salvia.

TROUBLESHOOTING TIP

When in doubt about whether a specific color will fit into your perennial garden, first try an annual flower with a similar hue. If it works, you can then replace the annual with a long-lasting perennial.

Perennials for All Seasons

One wonderful aspect of gardening with perennials is that there is a flower for every season.

Spring perennials are harbingers of a new garden year. Bulbs also present welcome color, but they do not offer the richness of foliage shape and form that early spring perennials do. Basket-of-gold *(Aurinia saxatilis)*, for example, bears its small golden yellow flowers above clumps of hairy, silver-green leaves. Spring perennials flower before pests and diseases have a chance to emerge from winter hibernations. In stature, they are often among the shorter perennials and many, such as Virginia bluebells *(Mertensia virginica)*, go dormant after flowering. The palette of spring colors—yellows, pinks, blues, and lavender pastels—is refreshing after a long dark winter.

Summer perennials are generally more robust and colorful than those of spring. Reds, oranges, and golden yellows appear at this time of year. You'll have the greatest number of species and varieties to choose from because summer is the best growing season in North America for most plants.

Unfortunately, summer perennials bloom at the same time that insects and viral diseases are at their peak and these pests can wreak havoc with a garden. While color, form, and texture are all important, choosing disease-resistant summer perennials should rank even higher—particularly if your border is large. Daylilies *(Hemerocallis)*, butterfly weed *(Asclepias tuberosa)*, black-eyed Susan *(Rudbeckia fulgida)* and yarrow *(Achillea millefolium)* are all exceptionally healthy plants for summer borders.

Fall perennials provide a lovely farewell to the garden year. Thanks to extensive breeding with asters and chrysanthemums, fall perennials now come in a complete range of colors. They too need to be tough to survive the heat and misery of summer and then

This woodland garden is the very essence of spring. Ferns, azaleas, and rhododendrons combine with bleeding-heart and phlox in shades of pink.

bear flowers. Fortunately, in the fall few insects are around to chew the blossoms once they open.

In winter, perennial gardens in all but the warmest climates lie dormant under their blankets of mulch and snow. Some perennials, such as perennial candy-tuft *(Iberis sempervirens)*, are evergreen in warm climates, where Christmas roses *(Helleborus niger)* and other early bloomers also provide winter color.

A summer theme expressed in pink, blue, and purple, clockwise from front right: bugleweed (Ajuga reptans), the pointed leaves of lemon verbena, spiky, blue veronica, soft pink beebalm (Monarda didyma), the tall globes of Echinops ritro, and rose-pink Phlox paniculata. The flower heads of sedum, still green, will come into their own later in the season.

One of the most interesting late-season perennials is Sedum × 'Autumn Joy'. Its flat flowerheads emerge pale green in midsummer, opening to light pink later in the season. As the flowers age, their color deepens to salmon (as seen here), then to an unusual coppery bronze, then deep russet. Good garden companions include golden-flowered black-eyed Susan (Rudbeckia fulgida) and silvery lamb's-ears (Stachys byzantina).

Perennials for All Regions

Regional Favorites

These regional natives will also shine in other locations.

From the West come British Columbia wild ginger (Asarum caudatum), *a ground cover for dry shade; a hybrid of coralbells* (Heuchera maxima × H. sanguinea 'Santa Ana Cardina'); *Silver King artemisia* (Artemisia ludoviciana *var.* albula 'Silver King'); *and Mexican evening primrose* (Oenothera berlandieri), *which bears lovely pink flowers in late spring.*

The Midwest is home to American columbine (Aquilegia canadensis), *which has red and yellow spurred flowers in early spring, and prairie blazing-star* (Liatris pycnostachya), *with spikes of lavender-purple flowers.*

Plants from the Southeast include green-and-gold (Chrysogonum virginianum), *with bright yellow flowers blooming in early spring, and obedient plant* (Physostegia virginiana), *with handsome pink flowers in late summer.*

The Northeast gives us black snakeroot (Cimicifuga racemosa), *which has elegant, soaring wands of white flowers in midsummer, and the colorful New York asters* (A. novi-belgii).

This typical Northeast garden includes bright pink phlox, lemony daylilies, yellow achillea, hosta, and 'Silver Mound' artemisia. A neat hedge and sculpture add elegant touches.

This Iowa garden features prairie flowers such as purple coneflower (Echinacea purpurea) *and drought-tolerant ornamental grasses.*

Shades of blue and gold shimmer in the soft light of this Oregon garden, which includes tall Verbena bonariensis, *shasta daisies, delphiniums, and golden* Coreopsis verticillata.

Neatly edged beds contain masses of spring color in this North Carolina garden. The pale blue flowers are woodland phlox (Phlox divaricata).

Succession of Bloom

Long-Blooming Perennials

The following star performers produce continuous flowers for two or more months.

'Moonbeam' Coreopsis (Coreopsis verticillata 'Moonbeam'). Pale yellow flowers that seem to float throughout wispy green

Wild Bleeding-Heart (Dicentra eximia). Abundant pink or white, teardrop flowers among handsome, blue-green foliage.

Purple Coneflower (Echinacea purpurea). Prairie native with purple, pink, or white petals around burnished copper cones.

Lancaster geranium (Geranium sanguineum var. striatum). Light pink flowers on low-growing, dark green foliage.

Other long bloomers are yellow corydalis (Corydalis lutea), balloon flower (Platycodon grandiflorus), feverfew (Tanacetum parthenium), and mallow (Malva alcea 'Fastigiata').

One of the most challenging aspects of designing with perennials is creating a succession of bloom. Even such renowned gardeners as Gertrude Jekyll and Vita Sackville-West often ended up designing perennial gardens that flowered for just one season. Among the seasonal gardens they designed were a spring bulb garden filled with bright blues, whites, and yellows; a magnificent long border filled with many summer perennials; and a fall garden composed of just one kind of plant—asters—in many different heights and colors.

Most people today have neither the space nor the time to create different gardens for each season. Rather, the goal is to have one garden filled with color throughout the growing period. Experienced gardeners know that it is almost impossible to rely solely on perennials to do such a job. To achieve all-season color you will probably need to incorporate bulbs and annuals in your garden.

If you choose plants carefully, an almost-all-perennial garden is easy to maintain and provides great variety throughout the season. As you plan for a succession of bloom, it is helpful to choose plants that flower for the duration of your favorite season.

Concentrate on the season that is most important to you. If you want your garden to shine in summer, plant spring bulbs or perennials, such as Virginia bluebells (Mertensia virginica), that go dormant by June. With such "disappearing" plants, the foliage and flowers of your summer plants will not be masked. And plan on setting pots of chrysanthemums in spots where summer bloomers such as red valerian (Centranthus ruber) have given up in fall. With these tactics, you'll have color in spring and in fall, and your garden will be packed with colorful plants throughout summer.

If fall is the season for you, grow bulbs in the spring and summer to pave the way for a glorious display of autumn perennials. Hardy spring bulbs and summer bulbs like flowering onions (Allium) take up little space and also go dormant, leaving no trace when your splendid fall flowers open up.

If you want a spring garden, include a few late-emerging perennials, such as hostas and Japanese anemones (Anemone × hybrida), that will flower long after some of your spring charmers such as Virginia bluebells and basket-of-gold have gone dormant.

Whatever your favorite season is, choose plants that flower for a long time. 'Moonbeam' coreopsis (C. verticillata 'Moonbeam'), for example, flowers from June through a light frost. Plants such as these provide some color in the garden during those quiet transition periods when other perennials have finished flowering and late-bloomers have yet to open up. Make sure these long-bloomers are prominently displayed.

With a little planning, it's also possible to achieve a succession of bloom over the changing seasons. One way to do this is to plant perennials by seasonal height. For example, plant spring-bloomers with handsome, low-growing foliage, such as hardy geraniums (Geranium species), in front of your perennial garden, interspersed with long-bloomers, such as yellow corydalis (Corydalis lutea). Plant medium-tall summer flowers, such as garden phlox (P. paniculata) and bellflower (C. persicifolia), in the middle of the border, and fall giants such as asters and boltonia in the back.

Finally, don't forget to incorporate colored foliage into your design scheme. Interesting leaves in purples, silvers, creams, and yellows can help make the garden attractive when little else is in flower. Heuchera 'Palace Purple' adds a splash of purple leaves to your garden.

Mixing Annuals and Perennials

TROUBLESHOOTING TIP

Generally, late spring is the best time to incorporate annuals into bare garden spots. When planted too early in the season, annuals may be crowded out by late-emerging perennials.

*I*t is a rare perennial garden that couldn't use an extra spark of color with the addition of annuals. Annual flowers have a bloom time that outlasts all but a few perennials. And since annuals must produce seed within their bloom period, they tend to be quite colorful and showy in order to attract insect pollinators.

Most gardeners rely on annuals to fill in the bare spots that appear when spring-blooming perennials go dormant. Annuals can also be used to create color in gardens that are going through transition phases, such as when summer-blooming perennials have finished flowering and fall charmers have yet to kick in.

Two deservedly popular annuals, impatiens and wax begonias, are staples in the shade garden. Both of these plants are nonstop bloomers and don't need to be pinched or cut back. They generally bear flowers in cool, soft colors—lavenders and pale pinks. If you want to heat up your shade borders, there are also varieties in magenta, orange, and red.

Two favorite sun annuals are marigolds and zinnias. Both of these plants need to be deadheaded often to maintain their vigorous bloom. Because there is such a ready market for these colorful plants, breeders have developed a remarkable variety of sizes, colors, and heights. In general, however, these are warm-colored plants.

As with perennials, annuals can be planted in formal groupings or in informal drifts. There are three general planting strategies for annuals:

▽ For continuous color in the garden, plant shallow-rooted annuals in areas left bare by spring perennials that have gone dormant by early summer.

▽ For the lushest growth possible, set aside specific areas of your garden just for annuals. Work in compost, humus, and fertilizers in the chosen locations before planting seedlings.

▽ Initially, plant annuals close together to get an extra boost of color early in the season. As they start to fill out and flower, weed out some of the plants.

Review design aspects such as height, width, and texture before incorporating specific annuals into your perennial borders. Snapdragons (*Antirrhinum majus*) and larkspur (*Consolida ambigua*), for example, are spiky plants that might provide the perfect contrast in a border filled with rounded, bushy perennials. Cosmos (*C. bipinnatus*) and the common sunflower (*Helianthus annuus*) are both garden giants, growing 6 feet and taller. Yet the first has an airy texture with its light green, feathery foliage and pastel, pink and white flowers, while the second is a bold plant with big leaves and huge, bright yellow flower heads that are up to 1 foot in diameter.

Annuals are usually sold with a few flowers in bloom, or a marker with a small picture of the flower's color, to indicate which color you are getting. It's best to buy annuals with unopened buds—they will adapt better to transplanting than plants covered with open flowers, and will bloom for a longer period of time.

Front-of-the-border annuals—impatiens, begonia, sweet alyssum, edging lobelia, petunia, ageratum, and nasturtium—blend well with perennials. Colorful candidates for the middle of the border include geranium, larkspur, flowering tobacco, yellow cosmos, scarlet sage, marigold, and zinnia. Tall annuals that liven up the back of the border include cleome, Mexican sunflower, hollyhock, cosmos, and sunflower.

For nonstop color all summer, plant annuals along with perennials. This striking border contrasts tall, deep blue delphiniums with bright orange marigolds. The plants shown below also mix well with perennials.

Larkspur (Consolida ambigua), *like other annuals shown here, combines beautifully with perennials. It's also good for cutting.*

The daisy flowers of Cosmos 'Sensation' come in various shades of pink, purplish red, and white.

Honey-scented sweet alyssum (Lobularia maritima 'Easter Bonnet') is an ideal edging plant, and is also lovely planted in drifts.

Salvia farinacea 'Victoria White' is often grown as an annual. 'Victoria' is an excellent cultivar with blue flowers.

Flowering tobacco (Nicotiana alata 'Metro Rose') blooms all summer in full sun or partial shade.

A Sunny Border Garden

*T*his lovely garden takes full advantage of a sunny location and features a collection of plants that provide a succession of bloom lasting through the spring and summer.

The primroses bloom in early spring, and as they die back, the coreopsis come in and fill the space throughout the summer with their sunny yellow flowers. In late spring the iris, geraniums, veronica, and columbine begin to display their color. Phlox, delphinium, daylilies, and most of the other blossoms arrive in the summer. The basket-of-gold and coreopsis will hold their bloom into the fall, as will the phlox in many regions.

Plant List

1 Japanese primrose
(*Primula japonica*)
2 Basket-of-gold
(*Aurinia saxatilis*)
3 Threadleaf coreopsis
(*Coreopsis verticillata*)
4 Siberian iris
(*Iris sibirica*)
5 Lemon daylily
(*Hemerocallis lilioasphodelus*)
6 Blood-red cranesbill
(*Geranium sanguineum*)
7 Perennial phlox
(*Phlox paniculata* 'Sandra')
8 Meadow rue
(*Thalictrum speciosissimum*)
9 Garden columbine
(*Aquilegia vulgaris*)
10 Black-eyed Susan
(*Rudbeckia fulgida*)
11 Shasta daisy
(*Leucanthemum × superbum*)
12 Catmint
(*Nepeta × faassenii* 'Six Hills Giant')
13 Speedwell
(*Veronica spicata*)
14 Candle larkspur
(*Delphinium elatum*)
15 Oriental poppy
(*Papaver orientale*)

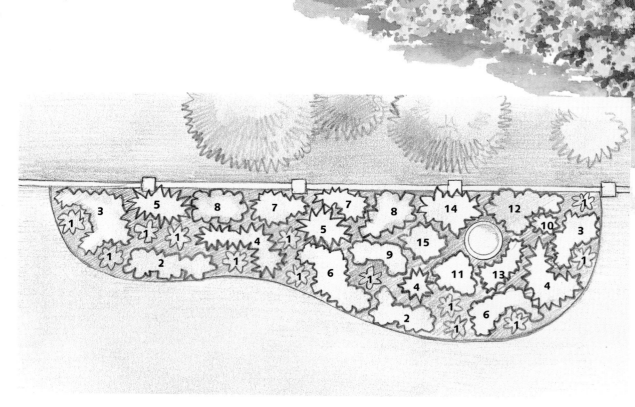

Pinching off flower heads—
called deadheading—will
help sustain the blooms of
many of the species in this
garden, including shasta
daisy, black-eyed Susan,
delphinium, and coreopsis.

Staking tall plants, such as
delphiniums, will help keep
them upright, particularly if
they are exposed to strong
winds and rain.

A Tiny Jewel Garden

*E*ven the smallest yard can contain a garden. This precious blue-and-white garden is inspired by the Blue Willow porcelain pattern. The inviting white bench is surrounded by fragrant violets and delicate forget-me-nots that keep on blooming through the summer. The shooting-star adds drama in the spring and then disappears, but the harebell will bloom into the summer.

Plant List

1 Moss sandwort
(*Arenaria verna*)
2 Wall rock cress
(*Arabis caucasica*)
3 Carpathian harebell
(*Campanula carpatica*)
4 Forget-me-not
(*Myosotis alpestris*)
5 Shooting-star
(*Dodecatheon meadia*)
6 Sweet violet
(*Viola odorata*)
7 Garden calla lily
(*Zantedeschia aethiopica*)

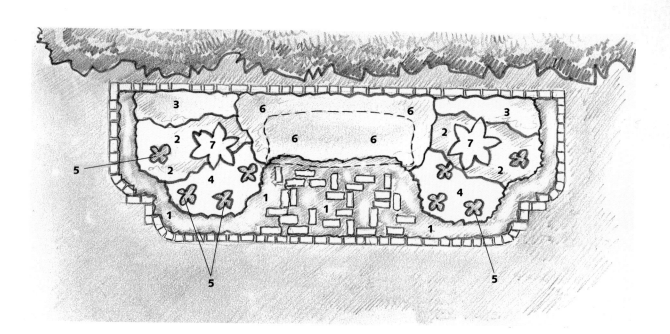

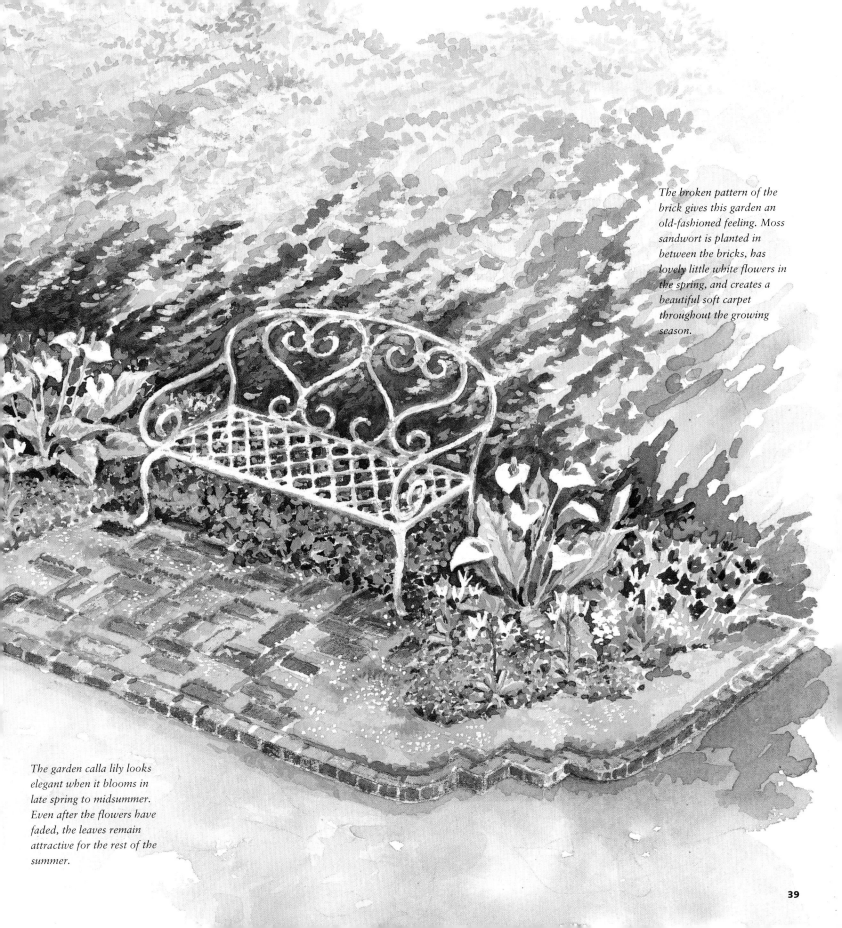

The broken pattern of the brick gives this garden an old-fashioned feeling. Moss sandwort is planted in between the bricks, has lovely little white flowers in the spring, and creates a beautiful soft carpet throughout the growing season.

The garden calla lily looks elegant when it blooms in late spring to midsummer. Even after the flowers have faded, the leaves remain attractive for the rest of the summer.

A Shady Corner Garden

*L*ush and woodsy, this shady corner garden makes the most of the filtered sunlight from the surrounding trees and shrubs. Liberated from the more common bed and border arrangements, this naturalized garden mixes ornamental with native vegetation.

This selection of plants shines in the spring, mimicking the time when woodlands are typically in flower. The delicate, starlike flowers of sweet woodruff give off a pleasant aroma. The bluestars look beautiful against the lushness of the ferns. The frothy white flowers of rodgersia bloom in late spring, and even after the blossoms have faded, the large and interesting foliage remains throughout the season.

Shady areas tend to have moist soils and are a challenge to gardeners. These problem areas can become beautiful focal points of the garden if you choose appropriate species.

Plant List

1 Black snakeroot
(*Cimicifuga racemosa*)
2 Queen-of-the-prairie
(*Filipendula rubra*)
3 Rodgersia
(*Rodgersia pinnata*)
4 Monkshood
(*Aconitum napellus*)
5 Blood-red cranesbill
(*Geranium sanguineum*)
6 Bluestar
(*Amsonia tabernaemontana*)
7 Maidenhair fern
(*Adiantum pedatum*)
8 Sweet woodruff
(*Galium odoratum*)

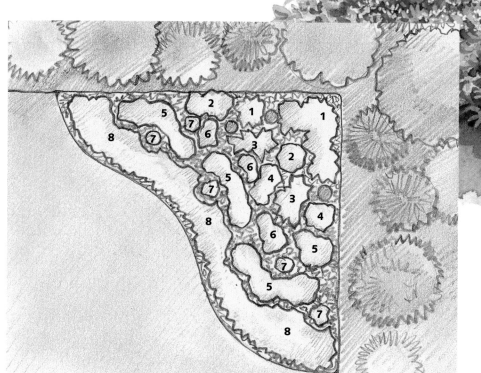

The spires of the black snakeroot and the monkshood are a nice vertical transition to the foliage of the shrubs and trees above.

A Cottage Garden

This garden provides a continual summer-long bloom for a variety of cut flowers. You needn't hesitate to pick a big bouquet of flowers every day from this garden. Cutting back the blossoms regularly will only encourage more blooms throughout the growing season.

Glorious blooms welcome friends and family in this charming cottage garden. The pathway to the front door winds through a profusion of flowers creating a colorful tunnel leading toward the doorway, which itself is softened by perennial pea growing up the porch columns.

Nothing about this garden is rigid or formal; it is a carefree collection of easy-to-grow perennials. Many are old-fashioned plants typical of Victorian-style gardens. They remind us of the simple pleasures of a bygone era and peaceful summers in the garden.

Plant List

1 Lamb's-ears
(*Stachys byzantina* 'Silver Carpet')
2 Inula
(*Inula ensifolia*)
3 Allwood pink
(*Dianthus × alwoodii*)
4 Rose campion
(*Lychnis coronaria*)
5 Blue-eyed grass
(*Sisyrinchium angustifolium*)
6 Lavender cotton
(*Santolina chamaecyparissus*)
7 Aster
(*Aster × frikartii*)
8 Hollyhock mallow
(*Malva alcea*)
9 Checkerbloom
(*Sidalcea malviflora* 'Sussex Beauty')
10 Threadleaf coreopsis
(*Coreopsis verticillata*)

11 Perennial phlox
(*Phlox paniculata* 'Sandra')
12 Candle larkspur
(*Delphinium elatum*)
13 Garden columbine
(*Aquilegia vulgaris*)
14 Boltonia
(*Boltonia asteroides* 'Pink Beauty')
15 Speedwell
(*Veronica spicata*)
16 Monkshood
(*Aconitum napellus*)
17 Foxglove
(*Digitalis purpurea*)
18 Perennial pea
(*Lathyrus latifolius*)

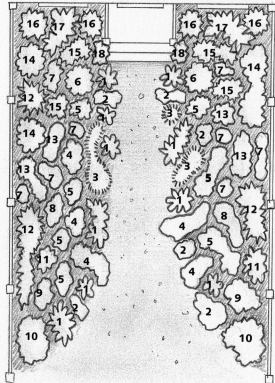

This garden contains several grayish plants, including rose campion, lamb's-ears, and lavender cotton. Their soft, silvery look works well with the other flowers and sets off the pinks, lavenders, yellows, and reds that brighten this cottage garden.

CHAPTER 2

Growing Perennials

*d*espite their beauty and variety, garden perennials have gained an undeserved reputation for being temperamental and difficult to grow. Nothing could be further from the truth. Indeed, many perennials are infinitely easier to maintain than annual flowers. • The key to success with perennials is to choose the right plant for the right place. This chapter presents guidelines on how to plant and maintain your perennial garden. Armed with these strategies, you can have a simple but colorful garden that requires no more than one or two hours of maintenance each week. Best of all, your plants will reappear year after year. • You'll also find the information you need to create more complex and stunning gardens. Although they will require more involvement on your part, such work need not be excessive if you follow the guidelines in this chapter.

Soil Care

EARTH·WISE
TIP

Many communities now give away one of the most effective soil conditioners: composted leaf mulch. This organic matter is an all-purpose additive that lightens clay soils by increasing drainage capability and thickens sandy soils by building up moisture retention. Call your local government to see how you can obtain this superb garden resource.

Perennials have adapted to every soil condition on the globe. There are plants that sprout from the clefts in rocks and others that arise from the muck of swamps. Perennials pop up along coastal sand dunes as well as wooded forest floors. Soil care depends upon the plants you choose for your garden.

One of the easiest garden practices is to plant perennials that already thrive in your existing soil conditions. If you find such a low-maintenance technique restricts your choice of flowers, you need to determine the kind of soil that exists in your chosen site. If the soil is thick clay (the kind used to make bricks or pottery), it contains many nutrients but can be so unyielding that roots may choke in it. Sandy soil, on the other hand, provides more room for roots to spread, but its porous structure allows all the nutrients to wash away.

You need to amend both types of soil by adding compost, humus, peat moss, and other organic material. Ideal garden soil drains within an hour after heavy rain, crumbles fairly easily in your hand, and is filled with essential nutrients. Working in organic matter each year will keep the soil in top condition.

You should also test your soil to determine its acidity or alkalinity, known as its pH level. The pH scale—measured from 1.0 for acid soil to 14.0 for alkaline soil—describes the degree of acidity or alkalinity of the soil. The soil pH affects the level of mineral nutrients available to growing plant roots.

The great bulk of perennials grown in this country flourish in soils with a pH ranging from 6 to 7. Acidic soil with a pH that measures below 6 can be adjusted somewhat with the addition of lime (this is called "sweetening the soil"). Similarly, you can lower a high pH by using a fertilizer intended for acid-loving plants, or mulching your garden with needles from pine trees. Trying to completely alter the pH of your garden soil, however, is a losing battle. Instead, seek out plants that grow well in the type of soil available in your garden.

Aloes, sempervivums, and other succulents need dry soil to thrive. This hillside is an ideal location.

Yarrow (Achillea) is an excellent plant for sandy soils and grows well in gardens near the sea.

Iris Pseudacorus flourishes in the wet, boggy soil along the edges of ponds and streams.

Most woodland flowers and ferns prefer humusy soil with an acid pH.

1 To prepare soil for planting a new garden, first remove the topsoil and pile it on a tarp. Mix compost or other soil amendments into the topsoil.

2 Loosen the soil in the bed with a spading fork and break up large clods. With your hands or a rake, remove stones and large weed roots.

3 Spread a 1- to 2-inch layer of compost or other amendments on top of the bed and dig it into the soil.

4 Place the amended topsoil in the bed and rake it smooth. The garden is now ready for planting.

TIMESAVING TIP

To cut down on soil preparation time, dig a deep, properly enriched hole for each plant rather than working the entire garden plot. To deter invasive weeds, make sure that all unworked areas are heavily mulched.

Light in the Garden

**Perennials
for Shady Places**

These perennials are among the hundreds that need shade to look their loveliest.

Lady's-Mantle
(Alchemilla vulgaris).
Sprays of tiny chartreuse flowers from spring into summer.

Goatsbeard
(Aruncus dioicus).
Soaring plumes of white flowers in late spring.

Pink Turtlehead
(Chelone lyonii).
Pink flowers in late summer.

Black Snakeroot
(Cimicifuga racemosa).
Towering spires of white flowers in summer.

Christmas Rose
(Helleborus niger).
Brilliant white flowers in late winter.

Virginia bluebells
(Mertensia virginica).
Rich blue flowers in early spring woodlands.

Primrose
(Primula spp.).
Sprightly pink, red, white, or yellow flowers in spring.

*J*ust as they have evolved to thrive in different soil, plants have also managed to find niches in different light conditions. Exotic desert perennials bake in the full glare of the sun throughout the day, while small woodland perennials may receive only an hour or two of dappled sunlight filtering through trees.

Light is a more complicated problem than soil, however, because light is an extremely variable factor. Light can be direct or indirect. Direct light describes conditions in which the sun's rays actually touch a plant. Indirect lighting occurs when the sun's rays first bounce off another object, such as the white wall of a building, or when they light up an area, such as a clearing in a woodland, without directly touching down on it. A woodland clearing would typically receive some hours of direct light and then a good deal more of indirect light.

Light conditions also vary by season and by time of day. Winter light, in the northern hemisphere, is a "low" light, because the sun is lower in the sky. The sun's rays slant under branches of evergreen firs and brighten up areas cloaked in dense shade during the summer months. Similarly, a house corner that faces northwest and is shaded throughout the winter months can be warmed by several hours of sunshine during summer when the sun is high in the sky.

Plants react differently to different types of sunshine, depending on the time of day. Morning sunshine, for example, tends to be cool and refreshing. It seems to waken plants from the quiet restfulness of the previous evening. Hot afternoon sun, on the other hand, contributes even more warmth to an area that might already have been parched by hot, dry weather.

Shade plants, such as hostas, can often tolerate three to four hours of early morning sun but will "burn" (the leaves will brown at the edges) if exposed to that much sun in the height of afternoon. On the other hand, sun lovers, such as New England asters *(A. novae-angliae)*, will flower quite freely with four hours of midday sun but will only bloom sporadically with a similar amount in the first hours of the day.

Light brings warmth with it. A building basking in summer sunlight often retains much of the sun's heat, and sometimes a corner will act as a heat trap. Temperatures can rise quite high in the afternoon, then decline by 10°F or more within an hour after sunlight ceases to shine on the area. Take care when planting perennials in these situations because they must cope not only with light, but also with intense heat in summer.

Dappled light, the kind that filters through trees, is an even more complex factor. Dappled or filtered light not only changes with the season and time of day, but also with changes in leaf growth of the trees overhead.

Since shade is so variable, then, experiment with your own light conditions. Although you might read that a plant is suitable for shade, you may discover that in your particular shaded spot it needs just a bit more light in order to thrive.

You can always help a plant adapt better to your garden by altering the light. In wooded areas, you can increase light by lopping off the lower limbs of trees or by thinning out shrubs. You can lighten the dark corners of a building by painting the building white or by adding reflectors in the form of brilliant white pebbles in an adjacent terrace or path.

In sunny areas, you can reduce the amount of light

Oriental poppies (Papaver orientale) *need plenty of bright sun. This open garden receives full, unobstructed sunlight all day.*

your plants receive. Trellises, arbors, and lath houses are ideal for shading plants and thus reducing the heat. These structures are often used in southern gardens to prevent heat-induced dormancy. Nature can also be used to reduce the amount of sunlight reaching your perennials, although this takes a little longer. Just plant a hedge or border of tall shrubs or small trees along the south side of the garden.

Some plants that like full sun in the North, such as the sedums and sempervivums tucked into this rock garden, will tolerate some shade in warmer climates.

Moisture

Perennials for Dry Climates

The following drought-tolerant plants grow well in a dry garden.

Yarrow
(Achillea millefolium).
Sun-loving flowers in white, yellow, or pink pastels on feathery, aromatic foliage.

Butterfly Weed
(Asclepias tuberosa).
Bright orange flowers in full sun throughout summer.

Yellow Epimedium
(E. × versicolor
'Sulphureum'). *Yellow flowers in early spring. Excellent for dry shade and poor soil.*

Flowering Spurge
(Euphorbia corollata).
Small white flowers on top of elegantly slim foliage; best in full sun all summer.

Blanket Flower
(Gaillardia aristata).
Showy yellow and red flowers throughout summer in full sun.

Showy Sedum
(S. spectabile).
Cool green succulent foliage with late-summer bright pink flowers.

A drought-tolerant garden combines ornamental grasses with perennials that go a long way on little water.

Changing weather patterns and increased suburbanization that drain the normal water table have made gardeners increasingly aware of how much water plants need. Just a decade or so ago, most gardeners could set up watering systems to supplement what nature did not provide. Droughts, however, have strained the delivery capabilities of water systems in places as disparate as California and New York City. An enormous number of plants have been lost in the dry years affecting both areas.

Sometimes nature seems to take a cruel delight in replacing a drought condition with torrential rains. Steady rainfall may be welcomed when the reservoirs need replenishing, but these same rains swamp plants that require dry conditions. In gardening it helps to be prepared for all eventualities!

Carefully consider the moisture conditions of the site you have chosen for your garden. Is it normal (as much as it's possible to define normal with today's chaotic weather), dry, or wet? Choose plants that do best in the prevailing conditions.

Plants that tolerate wet soil include Solomon's-seal (Polygonatum odoratum 'Variegata'), *ostrich ferns, and Japanese anemones.*

Perennials for Wet Places

Some perennials thrive in constantly moist settings, such as bogs or marshes. Marsh marigold (Caltha palustris), *turtlehead* (Chelone lyonii), *Kamchatka bugbane* (Cimicifuga simplex 'White Pearl'), *mallow* (Hibiscus moscheutos), *bigleaf ligularia* (L. dentata), *cardinal flower* (Lobelia cardinalis), *and Japanese primrose* (Primula japonica) *are all good choices.*

Some lovely irises like wet conditions. Louisiana irises (hybrids and species of Iris foliosa, I. fulva, I. giganticaerulea) *have flowers in many colors; 'Dorothea K. Williamson', a cultivar with wine-red blossoms, is the hardiest. The yellow flag iris* (I. pseudacorus) *has bright yellow flowers in late spring, and handsome, arching foliage wands.*

Next plan defensive measures to counteract a change in the moisture content. If the area you have chosen is dry, make sure the drainage is excellent. That way, even if there is excessive rain, the water should run off quickly. To increase drainage, dig out your garden bed to a depth of 1½ to 2 feet and install a drainage pipe. This will immediately carry away any excess water. Then refill the bed with enriched, porous garden soil filled with organic matter, such as peat moss and humus.

If your proposed garden area is moist, make sure you have the means to retain the moisture. Your garden should either be near a water source where you can sprinkle the spot daily or embedded with a soaker hose.

Or you can create your own miniature damp spot by following the techniques used to create garden pools. Simply install a container with a very small hole punched in for slow drainage. After you've filled the container, the moisture should seep out of such a setting at a very slow rate.

Planting Perennials

You can grow perennials from seed, from container-grown plants supplied by a nursery, or from divisions, cuttings, or layers made from established plants. Starting seeds and propagating plants by division and other vegetative methods are discussed in Chapter Three, "Propagating Perennials." Here we'll review some tips to keep in mind when planting seedlings and larger perennials in the garden.

Try to plant on a day when the weather is most congenial. Hot temperatures, burning sun, dry weather, and cold winds are all extremely stressful for new transplants. The best time to plant is on an overcast day when temperatures are mild and not likely to drop sharply at night. If you must plant on a hot day, do so in the morning or early evening. If the weather is dry, be sure to water well before and immediately after planting. If a chill wind is blowing, set up temporary windbreaks or shelters to protect the new plants.

Plant in groups, clumps, or drifts rather than dotting plants about the garden. You will create a more visually effective display by planting in groups. Odd numbers of plants generally produce a more natural effect than even numbers, which people tend to lay out in symmetrical patterns. In a small garden, plant three, five, or seven of a particular plant; in a larger garden, set out eleven or fifteen or even more.

Be sure to plant at the proper depth. Place container-grown plants at the same depth they were planted at the nursery. If you cannot tell how deep a bare-root plant was growing, find the junction of roots and top-growth, and position it just below the soil surface.

Remember to leave enough space between plants. When setting plants in their permanent locations, be sure to give them enough room to develop to their full mature size. Crowded plants lack vigor, flower

To achieve a natural look in a bed or border, plant in clumps or curved drifts that flow into one another.

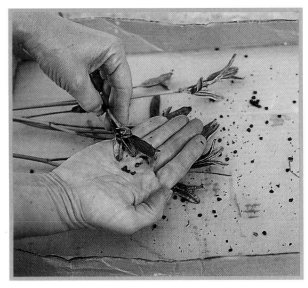

1 You can collect and save seeds from nonhybrid varieties, such as these Siberian irises, to plant next year. Clip off the seed pods when their color darkens.

2 Let the pods dry thoroughly, then shuck the seeds. Store the seeds in an airtight container in a cool, dry place. Label with the plant name and flower color.

poorly, and are more susceptible to attacks from insects and diseases.

Unfortunately, some people overestimate the number of plants that can fit comfortably in their garden. Many gardeners tend to be greedy when it comes to plant acquisition. They simply cannot resist growing new ones. They tend to send in large orders to buy plants through the mail or come home from garden centers with their car crammed with gorgeous plants in containers.

And then the box from the mail-order nursery is unpacked or the car is unloaded, and there is simply no room for the newcomers. These plants either must sit until a space is cleared or they must be stuffed into an already crowded garden. Not surprisingly, many of these new perennials do not survive.

Some perennials self-seed and pop up in the garden uninvited. Columbines *(Aquilegia species)*, forget-me-nots *(Myosotis scorpioides)*, and feverfews *(Tanacetum parthenium)* are particularly prolific self-seeding perennials. If ignored, the seedlings soon become a crowded mess in the garden.

These seedlings create ongoing problems for gardeners who cannot bear to throw away a healthy plant. Nevertheless, discarding self-sown plants is necessary for the health and appearance of the garden as a whole. Some of the seedlings can be transplanted to other areas of your property. The optimum time to do this is when the plants have two or three leaves; at this early stage of growth, they adapt easily to new surroundings.

Planting in Special Situations

**TROUBLESHOOTING
TIP**

*If in doubt as to which
perennials will succeed in
your stone walls, ask the
experts in your local Master
Gardener program. Under
the auspices of county cooperative extension agents,
these trained volunteers
answer horticultural questions and give advice about
local growing conditions at
no charge to the public.
You'll save both time and
money by planting only
perennials that are suitable
for your area.*

Structural elements such as stone walls and paths
help set the tone or mood for a garden. The English
refer to these structures as the "bones" of their beds
and borders. Creative gardeners often use these archi-
tectural elements as planting opportunities, allowing
flowers to decorate underlying structures.

Perennials that have evolved in rocky, mountainous
regions are popularly known as alpine or rock garden
plants. Many can grow easily in the cracks and nooks
of stone walls such as some species of rockcress
(Aubrieta), garden pinks *(Dianthus)*, and soapworts
(Saponaria). The flowers of these colorful plants naturally sprawl over stone walls while their roots flourish
in cool crevices away from the sun's glare. Just half-fill
with good garden soil, tap in your plant root, and
then pack in the remaining dirt.

Many perennials are particularly lovely when carefully placed along a path. Take care to ensure that
they do not overgrow the pathway.

One charming way to decorate a garden path is to
place fragrant herbs in selected spots. As they are
stepped on, the herbs release their pungent fragrance.
Perennials that can withstand such abuse include
chamomile *(Chamaemelum nobile)*, creeping mint
(Mentha requienii), and various thymes, such as lemon
thyme *(Thymus × citriodorus)* and caraway thyme *(T.
herba-barona)*. When creating your garden path, leave
open spaces for these shallow-rooted plants and make
sure that the drainage is excellent.

1 *When planting perennials in a dry stone wall,
first remove a stone to open up a suitable
planting space.*

1 *Small plants soften the look of a path. Dig a
planting hole between flagstones or remove a
brick from a brick path.*

2 With a long-bladed trowel, scoop out the soil from the planting pocket and mix it with compost or other soil amendments.

3 Position a small plant, such as this creeping sedum, in the hole and fill in around the roots with the improved soil mix.

4 Replace the stone, tapping it into place with the handle of the trowel. Water with a fine spray over the stone and adjacent plant.

2 Mix a trowelful of good-quality soil into the bottom of the hole. Remove the plant from its container, keeping the rootball intact.

3 Set the plant in the hole and fill in around the roots with enough ordinary soil or compost-enriched soil to anchor the plant.

4 When you have finished planting, water thoroughly, but with a fine spray that will not dislodge the new plants.

Planting Nursery Plants

*P*erennials bought at retail outlets, such as garden centers and hardware stores, and many plants purchased through mail-order companies, are usually packed in pots or cell packs. (Some mail-order plants are shipped bare-root. Planting bare-root perennials is discussed on pages 59-63.)

Potted perennials are described and priced by their pot diameter. A step-by-step guide for planting perennials grown in these pots is shown on page 57. Smaller containers (cell packs) are usually made of plastic and joined together in groups of four or six with each cell containing an individual plant. Sometimes cell packs consist of biodegradable material. That means you can set the plant undisturbed directly into the soil.

Perennials are also sold in undivided flats that are the size of six-cell packs. They generally contain many seedlings, which must be pulled apart before they can be planted; roots are often broken in the process. Unless you have no other choice, avoid buying perennials that are packaged in this manner.

Obviously, when you buy nursery plants through the mail you incur shipping costs. These costs are lower if the plant and the container are small; this is one of the reasons why most mail-order nursery plants are sold in cell packs rather than pots.

Container-grown perennials can be planted anytime during the growing season when the weather is not too severe. Plants adapt to the garden most readily when young, before they have buds or flowers.

1 Before planting container-grown plants, set out the plants in their pots to determine the best arrangement. Plants in asymmetrical clumps generally look most natural.

2 Dig a planting hole deep enough to hold the plant at the same depth it was growing in the container. Remove any rocks or root clumps obstructing the hole.

3 Gently slide the plant out of the pot, first tapping the bottom of the pot with a trowel handle to loosen the root-ball if necessary.

4 Set the plant in the hole and fill in around the roots with soil. Water; then add more soil if needed to completely fill the hole.

Planting Nursery Plants CONTINUED

TROUBLESHOOTING TIP

When ordering plants by mail, always specify a delivery date. That way, plants will not arrive when you are away. If you're unexpectedly out of town the week delivery is due, call the nursery and ask if it can delay sending the plants.

One advantage of buying plants from a mail-order nursery is that they often offer plants you can't find elsewhere. If you decide to order some little-known beauties through the mail, make sure the nursery guarantees that the plant is healthy and that it will arrive in good condition. Then follow the planting guidelines discussed below.

An advantage to buying from a garden center is that you can personally inspect the plants to make sure they are healthy and purchase them on the day you plan to place them in your garden. Don't buy perennials that display any of the following signs of disease or neglect:

▼ Yellow or wilted leaves—often an indication of illness or lack of water.

▼ Spindly stems—a sign that the plant has been growing in the pot too long.

▼ Many flowers—an indication that the plant has put most of its energy into blooms and may easily succumb to transplant shock.

▼ Weeds in the container—a clear sign that the plant is being robbed of nutrients.

▼ Roots crawling out of the pot bottom—another sign that a perennial has outgrown its container and is in a stressed condition.

Before planting your new perennials, water the seedlings so that the potting mix is firm and adheres to the plant. Then prepare a planting hole, remove the container (it can usually be snipped with scissors and then cut apart), and put the plant and its potting mix into the appropriate area. Place it as deep as the soil line in the container and fill in remaining gaps with garden soil.

Once the new plant has been placed in your garden, press down the surrounding soil so that it is firmly anchored in place. Gently water the area until it is well soaked. If you use a hose, make sure that the force of the water does not uproot your new flower.

Bare-Root Plants

When you order perennials through the mail you will most likely receive a bare-root plant that has been severely cut back. These plants have been grown in the field at the nursery. Before shipping, they are dug up and their roots are cleaned.

Bare-root plants are shipped while they are dormant. The roots are placed in a packing medium, and are then packaged in other containers for shipping. Why would anyone want to send plants in such an unattractive form? The answer has as much to do with politics as with horticulture. Bare-root plants do not have any soil about them; this eliminates disease-causing organisms and satisfies state laws governing imported plants. Plants without soil also weigh less and are less expensive to ship than plants growing in containers.

Bare-root plants are raised naturally in the ground rather than in a sterile, soilless mix in a container. Many horticulturists believe that outdoor growing conditions are best for plants because extensive roots can develop in unrestricted soil. The roots do not become cramped or twisted, as is often the case when perennials outgrow the small pots in which they have germinated.

Finally, bare-root plants tend to be more mature than perennials grown in containers, particularly the small ones grown in six-packs. It is possible to send these larger plants through the mail because they do not contain foliage and are not encumbered with a soilless potting mixture plus their container. Instead, these plants are usually packaged in damp, milled sphagnum moss and then wrapped in newspapers or placed inside breathable plastic bags. Their branches often have dormant buds, which spring to life as soon as the roots are placed in the ground.

Even knowing the merits of purchasing bare-root plants, many gardeners might find them both ugly and intimidating. What does one do with a mass of roots? A basic appreciation of a plant's root system will help you overcome any trepidation you may have about gardening with bare-root plants.

Roots are the internal subterranean engines of plants. They drive plants' initial growth and then work in conjunction with foliage to see that such growth continues.

When you receive a shipment from a mail-order nursery, unpack the plants right away and inspect them for damage. Water your new arrivals if you cannot plant them immediately.

Bare-Root Plants CONTINUED

There are two basic kinds of roots: taproots and fibrous roots. Both depend on root hairs—tiny extensions of their outermost cells—to collect water and nutrients in the soil and pass these on to the main root system.

Taproots continue to grow and elongate throughout a plant's life. Because all root functions are concentrated in one main growth, taprooted perennials are difficult to plant. Breaking off just one part of the root can sound a death knell to any future growth because it destroys so many of the root hairs. Carrots are probably the best known (and most colorful) example of a taproot.

Because of their fragility, bare-root perennials with taproots, such as butterfly weed *(Asclepias tuberosa)* and balloon flower *(Platycodon grandiflorus)* are sold as very young plants. The small root can be packaged and sent through the mail with less chance of damage than might occur with a larger, more mature root.

Fibrous roots are the underground equivalent of a heavily branched tree. These roots spread about throughout the soil, each tip covered with root hairs. Break off one of these tips and there are still many more to carry on the job. Thus, where bare-root plants are concerned, it is possible to mail mature fibrous-rooted plants, but not mature taprooted ones.

This does not mean field-grown, fibrous-rooted plants escape all injury. When they are dug, their fragile root hairs can be damaged. These need time to replenish themselves. If there is foliage on the plant, water will evaporate through the leaves. The damaged root hairs will not be strong or numerous enough to replenish this water loss.

1 *When you receive mail-order plants, unpack them immediately and inspect them carefully. Plants should appear healthy, with few broken or damaged roots.*

4 *Set the plant on the soil cone, adjust the height to position the plant at the correct depth, and spread the roots over the cone.*

2 *Dip bare roots in a bucket of muddy water before planting. Bare-root plants should have little top growth. Leafy plants like these should be cut back.*

3 *For a bare-root plant with fibrous roots, make a cone of soil in the bottom of the planting hole. Gently ease apart any tangled roots.*

5 *Fill in the planting hole with soil, carefully working it around the roots with your fingers. Fill the rest of the hole, gently press down the soil with your hands, and water well.*

**E A R T H • W I S E
T I P**

Add compost when you prepare the soil for planting a bare-root perennial. Avoid chemical fertilizers because they can be harsh and burn tender bare roots. Dip bare roots in a bucket of water before placing the plant in the hole.

Bare-Root Plants CONTINUED

In regions north of zone 7, spring is the preferred season for digging up and shipping fibrous-rooted perennials because foliage has not yet emerged and the cool growing conditions help plants settle quickly into their new home. Northern gardeners will almost always plant in spring as soon as the soil can be worked. In zones 6, 7, and 8 fall is also an acceptable time for planting bare-root perennials. In contrast to spring planting practice, cut the foliage of fall-planted perennials to the ground after planting. In zone 8, the weather in fall is mild and amenable for planting. Spring-planted perennials may suffer heat stress unless they go into the ground early.

When you receive a shipment of bare-root perennials, examine the plants carefully as soon as they arrive. The plants are supposed to be dormant, therefore you should not see much top growth. Look for firm, healthy buds on the crown, from which new stems and leaves will grow. If the plants have new shoots more than a few inches long, they are in active growth and no longer dormant. The plants probably suffered damage from cold weather during shipping and may have difficulty making the transition to the garden when you plant them. Check your plants'

Bare-root plants are packed in wood shavings, peat moss, or other material for shipping. Unpack nursery orders as soon as they arrive to be sure the rootstocks are in good condition, and be sure to keep the plant labels.

1 *Some bare-root perennials, such as this Siberian aster, have a long taproot and need to be planted in a deep, narrow hole.*

2 *Push a spade into the soil and move it back and forth to make the hole. Slide the taproot into the hole, check the depth, and press the hole closed. Water well.*

TROUBLESHOOTING TIP

Hot, sunny weather can devastate new transplants. When adding flowers to your garden under such conditions, try to ensure that the newcomers have some afternoon shade to help ease their transition into your garden.

crown and roots to make sure they are firm and healthy-looking. If they are dry and shriveled, or broken and damaged, return the plants and request replacements or a refund.

It is important to plant bare-root perennials promptly when you receive them. Most mail-order nurseries try to ship at the appropriate planting time for your area. If you can't plant right away, open the package as soon as it arrives, unpack and inspect the plants, and get the roots into water so they don't dry out. Set the plants in buckets of water deep enough to cover all the roots and let them soak overnight. Plant the next day if you possibly can, and keep the roots moist until you place the plant into the planting hole. After the overnight soaking, wrap the roots in plastic or wet cloths.

Review the photographs on pages 60, 61, and 63 to learn the basic procedures for planting bare-root perennials with fibrous roots and taproots.

Caring for New Transplants

No matter how carefully you have placed your perennials in your garden, these plants have nevertheless been uprooted during transplanting. They are in a state of shock, the degree to which is determined by the handling methods, and they will need some watchful care.

The photographs and instructions to the right illustrate how to make sure that your new transplants will succeed in your garden.

Your new plants must get enough water or they will die. Because it is inevitable that some of the root hairs were damaged in the replanting process, the remaining ones have to work overtime until new growth occurs. This means that for a good week or more the new transplants must be gently watered and the ground kept moist but not swamped—overwatering could drown a new plant.

Never directly fertilize a newly planted perennial. Ideally, the plant should not need fertilizer in subsequent weeks because it has been placed in enriched garden soil, where the necessary nutrients are already in place and available to the plant once the root hairs start to grow.

If you are transplanting tall perennials, such as delphiniums, it's a good idea to stake them at the same time. Staking helps the stem of a tall plant support its flowers once they begin to bloom; done at transplanting time, staking creates a minimum of disturbance for young plants. For detailed instructions on staking, refer to the step-by-step photographs and instructions on pages 72-73.

Check your transplants for signs of new foliage. This indicates that you have planted correctly and that your new perennial is surviving nicely in your garden.

1 *Water newly planted perennials regularly to keep the soil evenly moist, but not soggy, for the first week after planting.*

4 *In hot weather, shade the plants with floating row covers for the first few days after planting to ease their transition into the garden.*

2 Clip off any buds or flowers on bare-root plants; this precaution allows the plants to direct their energy into developing new roots.

3 Mulch with 1 to 2 inches of cocoa-bean hulls or other loose material. Mulch retains moisture and discourages weeds from growing.

5 After the plants are established, topdress with compost or fertilize lightly. Mature plants also benefit from a mid-season topdressing.

Maintaining Perennials

*I*f your garden is a reasonable size, has good soil, and contains low-maintenance perennials, you will probably need to spend no more than two or three hours a week maintaining it. Your chores will be divided into two kinds: ensuring the health of your garden, and maintaining its appearance.

Soil enrichment, pest and disease control, and other measures essential to garden care are discussed in other chapters of this book. After protecting your garden's health, your personal tastes will determine how much time you devote to making your garden look good.

Staking, reviewing color schemes, deadheading, and mulching are all garden beautifiers discussed in other sections of this chapter. To these garden-neatening chores you may wish to add pinching, a grooming practice that produces compact, bushy plants. To pinch a plant, remove the growing tip of a stem by nipping it between your thumb and forefinger. Each single pinched stem will divide into two stems.

Pinch spring- and early summer-blooming plants very early in the growing season. If you pinch too late you may inadvertently remove flower buds. The stems of late-summer and fall bloomers should be cut back—usually to no more than 1 foot—in late spring. Numerous side shoots develop from these shorn plants and eventually, these all bear flowers. Pinch fall bloomers, such as mums, no later than July; these plants need the end-of-summer growing season to set flower buds.

Pinching back branching plants like chrysanthemums once or twice while they are young encourages bushier growth and more flowers.

Plants grown for exhibition at a flower show need to be disbudded, staked to keep the stems straight, and scrupulously maintained, like these chrysanthemums.

To get bigger flowers on mums, pinch off (disbud) the side shoots so plants form fewer blossoms. These football mums reach maximum size when disbudded.

TIMESAVING TIP

While it is best to thin deeply rooted or woody plants in early spring or late fall, shallow-rooted plants, such as sundrops (Oenothera) and fern-leaf coreopsis, can be thinned at any time of the garden year. If they have overgrown their bounds, yank them out of your garden.

Good watering practices are one of the most vital ways to keep your plants healthy. If your plants do not receive adequate moisture, they will die. It is as simple as that.

Either a fixed or a portable watering system will get the job done. Fixed systems are built into your garden and are usually connected to timers so that your garden can be watered even when you are not there. Fixed watering systems can often be found in large public gardens. On the other hand, there are two clear advantages in using portable systems: they are cheaper than fixed systems and they can be moved to exactly where they are needed. Watering or sprinkling cans, hand-held hoses, and many portable sprinkler systems come under this category.

A good-quality garden hose is well worth the investment. When selecting a hose, look for four-ply construction, which provides superior burst resistance; a large diameter (5/8 inch is excellent), which allows water to be delivered faster; and brass couplings, which reduce leaks. When choosing a sprinkler remember that those made of brass and stainless steel last much longer than those made of plastic.

Newer watering tools, such as soaker hoses and other types of drip irrigation systems, are more water-efficient for home gardens. They are built into a garden and literally leak throughout the area in which they are placed. Since these systems are at soil level, the water goes directly to the roots and little is lost to evaporation. The easiest way to install soaker hoses is to lay them through the garden when plants are small, and cover them with a loose mulch.

Thinning and Deadheading

*T*hinning and deadheading are two measures that add to the good looks of your garden. Thinning refers to selectively eliminating plants or stems. The end result is a more attractive and healthier garden. (When thinning is carried out to increase the number of plants, it is called division; this procedure is reviewed in Chapter Three, "Propagating Perennials.")

If your garden contains mildew-prone perennials, such as phlox and beebalm *(Monarda didyma)*, you must ensure adequate air circulation to deter the formation of the fungus. This is simply a matter of periodically cutting enough stems to the ground so that

Summer phlox (Phlox paniculata) *is prone to mildew. To increase air circulation and decrease the chance of mildew, thin dense clumps, cutting some stems back to the ground.*

the remaining ones are not crowded. Such surgery in no way harms the plant. Thinning must be done regularly, however, because once mildew sets in it is hard to control without resorting to chemicals.

One easy way to thin plants is to inspect new shoots in the spring. If—as is often the case with phlox—they appear crowded together, simply cut out the woody center of each clump.

Other plants, such as veronica and lythrum, appear to be unaffected by crowded conditions. The garden may look messy, however, with these plants overgrown. In this case you may wish to thin the plants for the sake of appearance.

Deadheading is a grim-sounding term that describes cutting off the unattractive dead heads of flowers in your beds and borders. While deadheading is not essential, it certainly provides great rewards by prolonging the bloom period of most plants, preventing self-seeders from seeding, and ensuring a freshness and neatness in the garden.

Most plants are genetically programmed to produce seeds. Once seed is produced, the plant's function is completed, and it can appropriately wither or simply settle in as a foliage plant. If you cut the flower before the seed sets, however, the plant must produce another flower in order to fulfill its goal. The glory of modern breeding is the creation of sterile cultivars; these literally do not know how to stop producing flowers. If you wish to reduce deadheading in your perennial garden, choose sterile cultivars.

1 Garden phlox is susceptible to mildew, especially when the plants are growing in dense clumps. Although not usually fatal, mildew detracts from the plants' appearance.

2 To reduce the threat of mildew, improve air circulation by thinning out dense stands of phlox. Thin by simply cutting some stems back to the ground.

TIMESAVING TIP

Cutting flowers for indoor arrangements is a pleasurable way to deadhead many perennials, including feverfew, rose mallow, bee-balm, heliopsis, coral bells, veronicas, and stokesias.

1 When deadheading mums and other perennials, cut back the stem to the next set of leaves below the flower head.

2 Do not simply pick off the old flower heads, or the plants will be left with unattractive bare stems.

Cutting Flowers

One of the joys of gardening is that many of the perennials you admire outdoors can be cut and brought indoors. Here are some tips to follow when cutting perennials for an indoor arrangement.

▼ Use only sharp cutting tools. Dull blades will rip or tear a stem rather than give it a clean cut.

▼ Cut flowers when some but not all of the bud petals have opened. In general, the younger a flower, the longer it will last in an arrangement.

▼ Select only the healthiest blossoms for indoor decorations. Flowers that are damaged by weather or pests are not strong enough to handle the transition from outside and will soon wilt.

▼ Include as much of the stem as possible. Once indoors, stems can be shortened but never lengthened.

▼ Recut the stems after the flowers are brought inside. Cut the stems on a slant so that they can absorb water even when resting on the bottom of a container. Place the stems in water as soon as you recut them.

▼ Remove all foliage that will be underwater in the vase. If left on stems, leaves will rot and foul the water with bacteria.

▼ For the longest vase life, give your cut flowers fresh water each day, and cut about 1 inch off the bottom of the stems.

Remember that the foliage of perennials, such as wild bleeding-heart *(Dicentra eximia)*, Siberian bugloss *(Brunnera macrophylla)*, and hostas, can be beautiful fillers in arrangements.

Perennials for Cutting
Many perennials make fine cut flowers. The following flowers will live in a vase for at least five days.

Purple Coneflower
(Echinacea purpurea).
Purple, pink, or white petals encircle burnished copper cones throughout summer.

Globe Thistle
(Echinops ritro).
Metallic blue flowers resembling tightly packed globes of spikes in midsummer.

Creeping Jacob's-Ladder
(Polemonium reptans).
Small blue flowers in early spring slowly age to white in arrangements.

Gay-feather
(Liatris spicata).
Spikes of bright red-violet flowers in summer.

False Sunflower
(Heliopsis helianthoides 'Summer Sun').
Cheerful golden chrysanthemum-like blossoms throughout summer.

Lenten Rose
(Helleborus orientalis).
Pinkish purple flowers and handsome green foliage throughout spring.

Gooseneck Loosestrife
(Lysimachia clethroides).
White flowers in summer; nodding, odd-shaped blossoms resemble graceful swans.

Black-eyed Susan
(Rudbeckia fulgida 'Goldsturm').
Popular late summer flowers with golden petals and black centers.

'Autumn Joy' Sedum
(S. × 'Autumn Joy').
Garden staple with dusty pink flowers aging to rich brown-red in early fall.

Lady's-Mantle
(Alchemilla Vulgaris).
Fluffy sprays of chartreuse flowers from spring into early summer.

Staking and Fertilizing

*E*ven though they are grown in healthy soil and possess stout, sturdy stems, some perennials still need supports to help them stand tall and look their best. *Delphinium*, *Digitalis*, and *Thalictrum* are examples of plants that need staking to prevent them from crashing in high winds or strong thunderstorms. The examples on pages 72–73 demonstrate different support methods for perennials.

Fertilizer supplies your plants with mineral nutrients, an essential component of their diet. These nutrients are "fed" to the plant through the soil. Plants growing in soils that do not contain all the minerals show nutritional deficiency symptoms such as yellow leaves, floppy stems, or brown leaf margins.

Nitrogen, phosphorus, and potassium are the three big soil minerals and are called the major elements. They are followed by three minor elements—calcium, magnesium, and sulphur—and eight trace elements, which, as their name implies, are required in only minute quantities.

Most commercially available fertilizers contain only the three major elements packaged with inert filler. You can tell the proportions of each element by the number on the label. (The nutrients are always listed in alphabetical order.) Thus, a 10-10-10 fertilizer contains 10 percent nitrogen, 10 percent phosphorus, and 10 percent potassium. A 5-10-5 fertilizer, on the other hand, contains 5 percent nitrogen, 10 percent phosphorus, and 5 percent potassium.

It's easy to get stumped when deciding which nutrients to add to your soil since nutritional deficiency signs often resemble signs of disease. Furthermore, although nitrogen is essential for foliage growth, too much nitrogen can inhibit flower development.

In other words, fertilizer cannot be applied haphazardly to garden soil. When starting a new garden, have the soil tested by your county extension agent and get expert advice on just what essential nutrients need to be added. Once these nutrients have been incorporated into your soil, add generous doses of organic matter (compost) as mulch and sidedressings throughout the growing season. These steps should help keep your soil fertile.

Methods for incorporating fertilizers into your garden are demonstrated on pages 72–73.

To keep the tall stems of heavy-blossomed plants like delphinium (rear) standing straight, stake the plants when young.

Staking and Fertilizing CONTINUED

TIMESAVING TIP

Attempting to stake a mature plant can lead to broken stems. Where staking it is far better to err on the early side. Though the stakes may appear unsightly when surrounding a young plant, foliage soon covers them.

1 *Secure tall, straight-stemmed plants like delphiniums and lilies to stakes; use twist-ties or soft yarn in a figure-eight loop.*

2 *A metal stake with a loop at the top is another good support for straight stems. Put stakes in place when plants are small to help stems grow through the loop.*

1 *To apply a granular fertilizer, spread a handful of fertilizer in a ring around the base of the plant. To prevent burning, keep the fertilizer away from leaves and stems.*

2 *Scratch the fertilizer lightly into the surface, incorporating it into the soil, and away from the stems; then water well if the soil is dry.*

3 To support branched plants like these coneflowers, surround the clump with wood stakes, and zigzag sturdy string around and between the stakes to make a cat's cradle.

4 Support bushy plants like this young peony with a sturdy metal ring stake. These stakes are available from garden centers and mail-order suppliers.

3 Foliar feeding with a water-soluble fertilizer gives plants a midseason boost. Mix the solution according to package directions.

4 Apply the foliar feed with a watering can. You can also use a hose with a special attachment that dispenses the fertilizer as you water.

**EARTH•WISE
TIP**

When your perennials begin to emerge in the spring, circle them with a blanket of leaf mulch or compost. This not only enriches the soil each year but also smothers many annual weed seeds. As the garden season progresses, use dried grass clippings as additional mulch; these too will enrich your soil.

Weeding, Mulching, and Edging

*T*hree activities—weeding, mulching, and edging—ensure the neatness of your perennial garden. Do these tasks on a regular basis so the job does not become overwhelming or too time consuming.

Keep your garden free of weeds, as these persistent plants take up valuable soil nutrients, look messy, and crowd out other plants.

Mulch not only looks nice in the garden, it also helps control weeds and conserve water. When organic mulch is used, it will enrich the soil as well. Shredded leaves, dried grass clippings, buckwheat hulls, cocoa shells, shredded bark or wood chips, and finished compost are all excellent organic mulches. The first two are the cheapest and most readily available. The other mulches can all be bought at local garden centers and hardware stores. Woody mulches, such as uncomposted wood chips, cause a drop in soil nitrogen. These work best if they are composted before application. High-nitrogen mulches, such as grass clippings, may burn young plants. Avoid placing high-nitrogen mulches close to plant stems.

Edging is another excellent method for controlling weeds and keeping your garden looking neat and elegant. Edging creates a barrier to keep lawn grasses out of the garden and is also useful for containing spreading perennials.

TIMESAVING TIP

Use large foliage plants, such as hostas, to reduce weeds in your garden. The leaves from these plants completely shade the ground underneath them, preventing weed seeds from germinating.

1 *A mulch of loose material such as (clockwise from front) cocoa-bean hulls, shredded bark, compost, or wood chips helps conserve soil moisture and control weeds.*

2 *Spread 2 inches of coarse mulch or 1 inch of finer material around and between plants. The depth of the mulch depends upon the coarseness of the material.*

1 *An edging of brick gives a neat, defined look to a bed or border and separates the garden from adjoining lawn areas.*

2 *To install the edging, first dig a narrow trough around the perimeter of the garden. A flat-bladed spade works well.*

3 *To create a stable bed on which the bricks will rest, line the bottom of the trough with gravel or with sand.*

4 *Lay the bricks on top of the stone, pressing into the stone so that you are fitting the bricks together neatly and evenly.*

5 *To make a smooth corner on a curved bed, chip off the ends of a brick with a hammer to form an angled edge.*

6 *With both ends angled, the brick fits neatly into the corner. You may also need to angle the ends of adjoining bricks for a smooth seam.*

Pest and Disease Control

Vigorous plants growing in rich, loamy garden soil with the appropriate light and moisture generally don't have disease problems. However, despite your best efforts, some plants will succumb to disease and pest problems.

Controlling pests without using toxic methods is a greater challenge than preventing disease. Larger pests, such as deer, rabbits, moles, and squirrels, can only be deterred effectively with barriers, such as fences, wire mesh, or nets. Smaller pests, such as insects and caterpillars, are best controlled by using the integrated pest management (IPM) approach. The IPM philosophy combines cultural, biological, physical, and chemical controls, with the least toxic measures used first.

Cultural controls mean using good growing practices to raise healthy plants, keeping the garden clean, and planting varieties resistant to pests and diseases. It is also important to grow plants whose cultural needs match the conditions available in your garden.

Biological controls are exercised by encouraging beneficial insects, mites, or bacteria that prey on pests. A simple way to encourage beneficial insects is to include small-flowered plant species in your garden. Dill, caraway, lovage, and members of the *Compositae* family (coneflower, daisy, yarrow) all attract beneficial insects.

Physical controls include traps and barriers. Handpicking insects from plants is also an effective physical control.

Chemical controls—pesticides and fungicides in the form of sprays and dusts—should be the last resort. If you do use them, opt first for plant-based products such as rotenone and pyrethrum. Though highly toxic when applied, these materials break down quickly and do not last long in the environment.

1 *Solarizing soil before planting helps control nematodes. Cover the soil with a sheet of clear plastic for a few weeks. The sun's warmth, trapped by the plastic, will heat the soil.*

4 *Commercial slug baits lure the slimy creatures to their doom. Do not use baits where children or pets might be tempted by them.*

2 *Small insects like aphids can be washed off plants with a strong spray of water from a hose. Spray again with water or insecticidal soap if the pests return.*

3 *Larger insects, like Japanese beetles, can be picked off by hand if the infestation is not too severe. Crush the bugs or drop them into a jar filled with soapy water.*

5 *Gardeners who aren't squeamish can go into the garden at night with a flashlight to collect slugs by hand and destroy them.*

6 *At the first sign of disease, remove and discard the affected plant or plant parts. Do not put diseased plants on the compost pile.*

**E A R T H • W I S E
T I P**

Germs and viruses often strike plants through moisture on the foliage. Thus, using an overhead sprinkler to water a perennial garden bed is risky. Besides unneccesarily drenching leaves, the water emitted by overhead sprinklers takes a long time to reach and then soak into the soil where it is most needed. Instead of overhead sprinklers, use soaker hoses or other drip irrigation systems that deliver water directly to the roots.

Preparing for Winter

*I*n gardening, winter is defined as the time of year when most perennials become dormant. This time can vary from early September in some parts of the country to late December in others.

Cold is the major factor inducing plant dormancy. Thus, in preparing for winter, it's crucial to understand just what kind of cold affects your garden.

If chilly weather in your area means blankets of snow, you're in luck. Snow, sometimes called a "poor man's mulch," forms an insulating blanket on the garden. Temperatures in the ground beneath the snow cover always hover around 32° F while they can plunge far below 0° immediately above the snow line. Perennials that are dormant at a constant temperature rarely have trouble surviving winter months.

Plants in areas with little snow cover can suffer dreadfully during unexpected or unusual cold spells.

These need a 2- to 3-inch winter mulch—preferably an organic one, such as shredded leaves, pine needles, or licorice roots. The mulch protects plants from unusual cold spells and helps to maintain a uniform temperature so that the soil does not thaw out prematurely or expand ("heave" in garden terms) when encrusted with frost and ice particles.

Before you add mulch in winter, however, make sure your garden bed is as clean as possible. Clear away dead foliage and destroy all weeds. Spread the mulch just after the soil freezes.

Now, step back and take a look at your pristine garden. If you have been considering improvements, decide where you would like to place new perennials and put markers in these areas. If possible, write the name of the intended plant on each marker; this will make spring planting much easier.

1 *To prepare perennials for their annual winter dormancy, cut back the stems to a few inches above the ground. Clear away the dead foliage.*

2 *When the ground freezes, mulch plants with several inches of hay, shredded leaves, or other loose material, to prevent soil heaving.*

In cold areas, perennial gardens rest in winter. Here, only the garden's "bones"—shrubs, trees, and benches—stand out under the cover of snow.

Ligularia tussilaginea *blooms in early January in this Southern California garden. Polyanthus primroses (Primula × polyantha) are beginning to bloom along the sidewalk.*

Before shutting down your garden for winter, have your soil tested. Just call your local county cooperative extension agent and ask for instructions. A soil test will give you information on the pH (acidity) of your soil plus suggestions for any additives needed to improve fertility. Correcting any soil deficiencies now will make spring planting easier and smoother.

Regional Calendar of Garden Care

 Spring ❋ *Summer*

COOL CLIMATES

Spring

- Gradually begin to clear your garden of its winter mulch as soon as night temperatures rise above 30°F. Overcast, windless days are ideal for performing this task.

- After removing mulch or leftover debris from the fall, pull out weeds wherever you find them; if you question whether a plant is a weed or a flower, leave it in place.

- Buy healthy plants with sturdy growth, unblemished foliage, and no open flowers. These will adapt quickly to your garden.

- Prepare the soil by mixing in organic material before adding plants. Start planting new perennials in your garden beds.

- Divide or thin summer- or fall-blooming perennials that have become crowded. Transplant the extra flowers to new garden beds.

- To keep them erect, stake tall perennials before plants are 1 foot tall.

Summer

- Cut back faded flower heads that are past their prime. Many of these contain seeds. If you want them to self-sow, leave the snipped flowers on the ground. Compost the spent flowers if you want to contain their spread.

- Cover open spaces with mulch to smother annual weeds, conserve moisture, and enrich the soil.

- Plant annuals in bare spots. Try to have these colorful flowers flow through your garden in drifts.

- Forcefully spray any insect-infested plants with water or insecticidal soap early in the morning. This is particularly effective when combatting aphids and mites.

- Discard any plants that show signs of disease. Don't put affected plants on the compost pile.

- Apply an all-purpose fertilizer to long-blooming perennials that are flagging in mid-summer.

WARM CLIMATES

Spring

- Install a soaker hose or drip irrigation system if they are appropriate methods of watering your garden.

- Use soil polymers to combat drought conditions. These tiny granules significantly aid the moisture-retaining capabilities of your soil.

- Save dried lawn grass clippings and use them to mulch your flower beds.

- Deter pests, such as aphids and spider mites, by spraying any stricken plants with a water hose early in the morning. If a forceful spray of water doesn't work, try an insecticidal soap. An immediate, low-toxicity approach can effectively prevent the build-up of large insect populations and the need for more lethal sprays.

- Eliminate weeds quickly before they have a chance to spread.

Summer

- Add annuals to your garden if your perennials are suffering from intense summer heat.

- Deadhead spent flowers regularly unless you want plants to self-sow.

- Check your plants constantly for signs of water loss. The higher the temperature, the more water a perennial will lose through evaporation. Water at soil level so the moisture will go directly to the roots where it is needed. Keep the garden well mulched.

- Keep lower leaf surfaces properly drenched when spraying for insect infestations. Watch for signs of disease and promptly remove any affected plants.

- Late summer is an excellent time to direct-seed perennials. Give the tender young seedlings adequate moisture and some protection from hot sun during midday.

Fall

- Clean perennial beds and borders thoroughly. Cut down and rake off dead plants. Dig up and remove all diseased plants. Weed ruthlessly.

- Continue planting perennials, especially those that bloom in spring. Plant in the fall so the roots have time to acclimate before winter.

- Visit end-of-season sales at local garden centers. Before taking advantage of great bargains, however, make sure the perennials are suitable to your garden and will fit into your design scheme.

- Set up a compost area for your healthy garden refuse if you haven't done so already. Don't compost weeds that have gone to seed.

- Thoroughly clean all garden tools before storing them for the season.

- Build a coldframe to overwinter marginally hardy perennials and to harden off perennials you grow from seed during the winter months.

- Continue checking your plants for outbreaks of aphids, whiteflies, and leafhoppers. Take immediate control measures when these pests appear.

- Give your perennial beds and borders a thorough housecleaning in late fall. Cut down and rake off dead plant material. Remove all diseased plants and weed ruthlessly.

- Divide overgrown clumps of spring- and summer-blooming perennials. If you don't have room for your increased stock, share with friends.

- Rework garden beds and move plants around to better fit your design schemes. Continue planting new perennials in early fall, so the young plants have time to establish their roots before winter dormancy.

- Plant pinks *(Dianthus)* and pansies *(Viola).* These colorful perennials will often bloom throughout winter and into early summer.

Winter

- Continue your horticultural education inside since you can't tend to the garden outside. Visit flower shows, learn about new plants by reading mail-order nursery catalogues, and search for good books to add to your garden library.

- Grow perennials from seed. This is the cheapest way to obtain new plants and the only way to obtain many rare ones. Order seeds now from retail firms or plant societies and start them indoors.

- Avoid using salt or salted sand to melt ice near your garden beds and borders. The salt will leach into the soil and destroy your plants.

- Cut up evergreen boughs and trees used as holiday decorations. These make an excellent and inexpensive garden mulch.

- Use row covers, sheets, or old blankets to protect your perennials during a heavy, severe frost.

- Check nearby shrubs for any signs of overwintering masses of insect pests. Remove the egg sacs before they have a chance to hatch.

- Mulch the soil with the organic matter you have been composting during the year. This will enrich your soil and break down even more so that it won't impede the growth of emerging perennials in spring.

- Analyze your soil. Contact your local county extension agent for instructions on how to do this.

- Throughout winter-dreary days pursue your garden education. Visit flower shows, learn about new plants by reading mail order nursery catalogues, and search for good books to add to your garden library.

This table offers a basic outline of garden care by season. The tasks for each season differ for warm and cool climates: warm climates correspond to USDA Plant Hardiness Zones 7 through 11, and cool climates to Zones 2 through 6. Obviously, there are substantial climate differences within these broad regions. To understand the specific growing conditions in your garden, consult the Zone Map on page 127. Also be sure to study local factors, such as elevation and proximity of water, that affect the microclimate of your garden.

CHAPTER 3

Propagating Perennials

*t*he easiest way to acquire perennials is at a garden center or through the mail. Unfortunately, it is also the most expensive way to obtain plants—especially if you have a large garden. • Buying plants from retail outlets is restrictive as well, because these sources may only offer popular plants or ones for which they can easily create a demand. Gardeners with limited budgets or a hankering for the unusual should propagate perennials in order to grow the quantities and kinds of plants they want. • In addition, many perennials grow so vigorously that they form large, crowded clumps which bear fewer and fewer flowers. By learning how to divide these plants properly, you will boost the health and flowering of your perennials. • Not only will you gain additional plants for other parts of your property, but you'll also have more plants to swap with friends and neighbors.

Growing from Seed

Growing perennials from seed is inexpensive, and allows you to obtain rare and unusual plants. You can direct-sow perennials outdoors when weather conditions are suitable, or you can start the plants inside. Let's take a look at indoor seeding.

A plant seed is a miraculous object. It contains all of the necessary nutrients and genetic instructions to nurture the new seedling for a week or two after germination. That means you don't have to fertilize during your initial seeding. Always use sterile trays or containers and a sterile potting mix to reduce the chances of disease.

Seed germination times and light requirements vary considerably. Some seeds sprout in direct light in less than a week; others require a month or more of darkness. Therefore use separate containers, grouped by light requirement, for the various perennials you are seeding.

Seeds also vary in their depth of planting requirements. Planting depth is usually provided with the seed packages. A sharpened pencil is often a handy instrument for making seed holes in a prepared mix.

Never directly water a planted seed tray or container until germination occurs. Rather, use the indirect method; water through drainage holes located at the bottom of each seed container. Place containers in a tray of water deep enough to cover the drainage holes until the soil surface feels moist. You can cover seed trays with plastic tops to create a terrarium-like setting, where moisture is constantly recycled.

Winter is usually the best time to start perennials from seed. This is a particularly rewarding endeavor for those living in bleak landscapes at this time of year. It is a great thrill when the seeds start to germinate and a fresh, green plant emerges.

1 *A light, porous potting mix is best for starting seeds indoors. Add perlite or vermiculite to potting soils to lighten the texture and improve moisture retention.*

4 *Press seeds lightly into the surface of the medium. Mist with a fine spray to avoid dislodging the seeds, or set containers in a pan of water until the soil surface feels moist.*

2 Fine seeds can be difficult to handle. To make it easier to distribute them evenly over the soil surface, mix tiny seeds with an equal volume of sand before sowing.

3 Scatter seeds as evenly as possible over the surface of containers of moist potting medium. Use your fingers, or tap seeds from a spoon or a folded piece of paper.

5 Cover containers with plastic to keep the humidity high. Keep them out of the sun until seeds germinate, then remove the plastic and give seedlings a lot of light.

Transplanting Seedlings

A plant's first leaves after germination are called cotyledons; true leaves are the green foliage that develops after these, and are an indication that root growth has begun in earnest. Once a seedling has at least four true leaves, you can transplant it into either a larger pot or a permanent home outdoors. If you are not ready to put your seedlings outdoors, it is best to give them more growing room inside.

The first step is to discard the weaker seedlings and gently lift the more robust ones so little or no damage is done to the root hairs. Carefully place these stronger seedlings in new containers of sterile potting mix. Gently cover the roots with the potting mix and firmly pat all in place. Include a light application of liquid fertilizer when watering.

If you want to plant seedlings raised indoors directly into their garden homes, harden them off for approximately one week prior to transplanting. To accomplish this, place them outside in bright but indirect light. This gives them time to acclimate to uneven temperature and light conditions. Set the plants outdoors for just a few hours the first day; then lengthen their time outdoors a bit more each day, finally leaving them out overnight before transplanting.

When it comes time for the actual planting, dig a hole that is slightly larger than the container in which your seedling has been growing. Then follow the step-by-step photographs and instructions shown to the right. If you place your seedlings into fertile soil, you should not need to add fertilizer at this time.

1 *A few days before transplanting seedlings to individual pots, block the soil in undivided flats. Slice the soil into blocks, with each seedling in its own block of soil.*

1 *When seedlings are several inches tall and have developed sturdy root systems, they can go into the garden. These plants are growing in a flat separated into individual compartments.*

2 When transferring the seedlings to individual pots, hold the plants by the uppermost leaves, not the stems. Support the roots with your hand or a teaspoon.

3 Move the pots of seedlings to an outdoor nursery bed or empty cold frame during warm weather. If weather is still cold, put the seedlings under plant lights or on a sunny windowsill.

4 In hot weather, cover the seedlings with a suitable length of shade netting for several days to help them adjust to outdoor conditions. Netting is available at garden centers.

2 Carefully remove the plants from their containers (a wooden stick is a handy tool) and set them on top of the ground where you will plant them.

3 Quickly get the plants into the ground before their roots have a chance to dry out. Plant at the same depth the seedlings were growing in their containers.

4 Water the plants thoroughly, and as needed thereafter to keep the soil evenly moist—but not soggy—for a week as the plants establish themselves. Mulch to conserve moisture.

Tip and Stem Cuttings

Many plants can't be propagated by seed because they are either sterile hybrids or cultivated varieties that do not breed true. In these cases, tip and stem cuttings, which produce an exact clone of the parent plant, are often the best means of propagation.

A tip cutting, as its name implies, is taken from the end of a stem; a stem cutting can come from any part of a stem. For prolific production, it's possible to cut one stem into many pieces and root each piece.

Speed is essential when propagating with stem cuttings. Just as some flowers wilt shortly after being cut, so do stems. They need to be placed in their prepared growing medium as soon as possible.

Whether you take one or more cuttings from a stem, be sure to slice each just below a point called a node, the area where a leaf joins the stem. In order for the stem to take root, it must have at least one node—but it can have more if you wish.

Clean the stem of any leaves below the node. Many gardeners like to dip the stem into a hormone rooting powder to increase the possibility of success; others feel this is unnecessary or varies with the kind of perennial being rooted. In any case—dipped or undipped—place the cleaned stem in a potting mixture, generally composed of equal parts moist peat moss and coarse sand. Position the node just above the soil line.

Unlike seeds, tip and stem cuttings are directly watered. Either cover them with plastic and place them in a terrarium-like setting, or check them periodically and water directly if they become dry.

Cuttings need light, but not hot beating sun. Grow them either under plant lights indoors or outside in very bright, open shade.

1 *Take tip cuttings from the ends of healthy stems, cutting just below a node. For dianthus, shown here, cuttings are taken in summer.*

5 *Insert the bottom of the cutting into a pot or flat of moist, light rooting medium, such as a mix of peat moss and perlite.*

2 Make stem cuttings 3 to 6 inches long. Work quickly when you handle the cuttings because they wilt rapidly.

3 Carefully remove the lower leaves from each cutting in order to expose a couple of inches of bare stem.

4 Dip the bottom of the cutting into rooting hormone powder. Pour a little powder into a container, and discard the excess later.

6 In the flat, place the cuttings close together but not touching. Transplant them as soon as they root.

7 Cover the flat with plastic to maintain high humidity. Open the plastic briefly each day to check soil moisture and let in fresh air.

Root Cuttings

*D*andelions are probably the best-known example of a plant that is easily propagated by root cuttings. To many a homeowner's despair, just one deeply buried root tip remaining from a pulled plant quickly rejuvenates itself into a full-grown pest. Unfortunately, most perennials are not as easily propagated by root cuttings as dandelions. Root cuttings should be used to increase a plant's stock only when other methods are not practical.

To propagate by root cuttings, lift up the dormant plant and snip off a 3- to 4-inch section of the root. First make a straight cut near the crown; then make a slanted cut at the outermost area of the root.

Place an extra inch or more of growing medium at the bottom of the container to give the root tip room to spread. Place the cut root vertically in a container, with the flat-cut end at the top. Fill the container to the top of the cutting with a moist, well-drained growing medium, such as a mix of peat moss and coarse sand. Cover the top of the root with a thin layer of sand or vermiculite no more than 1/2 inch thick.

Root cuttings do best in cool surroundings; therefore don't attempt this procedure in the height of summer. Depending on the variety of perennial, early spring or late summer into fall is the best time to do this type of propagation. Common bleeding-heart *(Dicentra spectabilis)*, for example, goes dormant after spring bloom, so its root cuttings should be taken at the end of the garden season.

After the cut roots have been potted, place them in a cold frame or an unheated greenhouse. Give the new plant lots of bright, indirect light, but keep direct light to a minimum. As with other forms of propagation, keep the root cutting moist but not drenched. Check the soil for moisture and water as needed.

Perennials to Grow from Root Cuttings

The following can all be propagated from root cuttings:

Bear's-Breech
(Acanthus mollis)

Italian Bugloss
(Anchusa azurea)

Butterfly Weed
(Asclepias tuberosa)

Siberian Bugloss
(Brunnera macrophylla)

Persian Cornflower
(Centaurea dealbata)

Common Bleeding-Heart
(Dicentra spectabilis)

Gas Plant
(Dictamnus albus)

Oriental Poppy
(Papaver orientale)

Stokes' Aster
(Stokesia laevis)

Mullein
(Verbascum bombyciferum)

1 *To propagate plants like this oriental poppy from root cuttings, first dig up the plant and hose off the roots to remove soil.*

4 *Cut the roots into pieces that are 2 to 3 inches long, again sterilizing the knife after every cut in the same solution used in step 3.*

2 Carefully cut apart the root mass or, if you want to save the parent plant, cut off a clump of roots and then replant the parent.

3 Cut apart and save healthy roots ¼ to ½ inch in diameter. After each cut sterilize the knife in rubbing alcohol or a solution of 1 part chlorine bleach to 9 parts water.

TROUBLESHOOTING TIP

When working with root cuttings, plant the end nearest the root crown at top. If you can't figure out which end is which, place the root horizontally in the growing mixture. Nature will eventually take over and send down roots at the appropriate end and push the emerging foliage above the soil.

5 Soak the root cuttings in a fresh container of the diluted bleach solution for a minute to destroy any pathogens that may be present.

6 Place the cuttings horizontally in containers filled with light, sterile rooting medium. Set the cuttings close together and cover with ½ inch of soil.

Division

*D*ivision keeps your plants looking their best, and is the easiest and most reliable way to increase your perennials. Like taking root cuttings, division produces plants that are clones of the parents.

If you're dividing plants to increase your stock, do so in early spring. That way you can separate the roots that have been quietly resting over winter, and because these plants are just starting to grow, division will not be much of a shock to their system.

Divide your plants on a cool, overcast day. Cool, sunny days are fine, but hot, muggy days are not. When you don't have the luxury of waiting for the right weather, work in late afternoon or early evening. The relative coolness of the evening will help your plants adjust to their surgery.

Prepare the soil in an appropriately sized new space for your divided plants. Dig a hole about twice the depth and diameter of each plant's roots. Check the drainage of the soil and if necessary, add peat moss, sand, or other soil conditioners to the new hole and the current location after you've removed the established perennial.

Check the root structure of the plant being divided and then plant the separated parts appropriately. For example, the roots of coral bells (*Heuchera* spp.) are shallow and spread out just under a top layer of soil. Peony roots, however, are large and burrow deep into the garden. When dividing these plants, the buds (or "eyes") on the top part of the root should rest 1 to 2 inches below the soil surface. (If planted too deep, peonies will not bloom.)

Be sure to water thoroughly after planting each division, and continue to do so for at least a week or until the plant settles in and resumes foliage growth.

1 *The first step in dividing a crowded clump of perennials is to get the clump out of the ground. Dig vertically around the outside of the clump.*

4 *To make it easier to see what you are doing, it is helpful to hose off the plant in order to remove most of the soil from the roots.*

2 Push a shovel or fork on an angle under the root ball, and lever it up and down to loosen the roots. Lift the clump out of the ground.

3 Once the clump of roots has been pulled from the garden, gently shake or brush excess soil from the entire root ball.

5 Pull, cut, or pry apart the clump into smaller sections. Discard the old, woody central part of the root clump, and save the young outer sections.

6 Be sure all the divisions have both roots and growth buds, or eyes. Replant them immediately, before they begin to dry out. Water well.

EARTH • WISE
TIP

The summer beauty of perennials, such as garden phlox and bee balm, is often marred by a disfiguring, powdery white mildew. If these plants are divided in early spring— even though they don't appear to be crowded— enough air should circulate among the divisions to discourage or even eliminate the ugly disease.

Division CONTINUED

Division is also essential in maintaining the health and vigor of many perennials. A dying middle section, decreased flowers, and large clumps all indicate that a plant needs to be divided.

In general, division to maintain plant vigor takes place soon after blooming is finished. Thus, over-crowded spring perennials are divided in midsummer, summer perennials in fall, and fall perennials with the first flush of growth the following spring. As you are dividing, it is a good idea to leave some of the plant in its original place as protection if the divisions die.

When dividing a plant for rejuvenation, plant growth patterns influence the tools and methods used for the division. Sometimes the center of the plant becomes so thick and woody that it can no longer put forth abundant foliage or flowers. Depending on the size of the plant, use a trowel, a spade, or a hatchet to cut out and discard the tough, nonproducing inner part. The resulting plant will look like a doughnut, which you may treat in one of two ways.

One option is to lift the entire plant from the ground, break its round, doughnut-shaped structure into sections (each section containing a minimum of two or three stems), and plant these sections to resemble the undivided plant. Or, if you want to leave the plant pretty much as it was originally growing, carefully cut a chunk of the plant—roots and all—from the outer ring and replant it in the vacant center.

Other plants, such as coral bells, have intertwining fibrous roots that form a dense mass. Those on the bottom of the heap suffer and those on top often lose contact with soil. Dig up the whole plant with a shovel or trowel and gently tug the roots apart or cleanly sever them with a sharp knife.

Still other plants, such as Siberian irises and daylilies, tend to become packed into dense overgrown stands, causing a reduction of blooms. Dig up the entire clump and insert two digging forks, back to back, in the center. Pressing outward on the handle of each fork, pry the plant apart. If the center of the clump is thick and woody, discard it. Depending on the size of the clump, each half can then be similarly divided.

Rapidly spreading plants, such as sundrops (*Oenothera fruticosa*), can really be a problem. Most of these spreaders are shallow-rooted and are easily yanked out by hand or with a trowel. In this case you are actually thinning rather than dividing.

Since division usually occurs shortly after the bloom period, the plants are equipped with abundant foliage. It's hard to support both this growth and the shock of garden surgery. Give each division a crew cut, leaving all stems just 1 to 2 inches high. This allows the plant to acclimate itself to a new setting, and you don't have to worry about the growth of foliage.

Some of the plants in this mature garden will soon need division. When plant clumps become crowded, bloom quality and quantity decline. It's also time to divide when the center of the clump looks empty.

1 To propagate a parent plant, make smaller divisions for a nursery bed. They will take longer to reach blooming size but will produce many more plants.

2 Plant the divisions at the same depth they were growing when attached to the parent. If in doubt, position with the crown—where roots meet stem—at soil level. Water well.

3 In a hot, sunny location, erect a shade canopy of a floating row cover supported by corner stakes over the nursery bed.

4 Finally, cut back the top growth of the plants in order to reduce the moisture loss and also encourage new root development.

TROUBLESHOOTING TIP

Division, rather than transplanting, is often the best method of moving large, mature perennials. It is difficult for large, established plants to adjust to transplanting; a small division has a much better chance of successfully settling in.

Perennials for American Gardens

This section provides concise information on more than 150 perennials recommended for American gardens. The plants have been selected on the basis of beauty, adaptability, and availability. If you're looking for plants for particular uses—of a certain height, for instance, or with flowers of a certain color—look first at the Color Range and Growth Habits columns. If you need plants for a shady spot, look at the Growing Conditions column. Or you might prefer to look at the photos, read the descriptions, and then decide which flowers will grow well in your garden. Each photograph shows a species or variety described in the entry.

▼ About Plant Names

Plants appear in alphabetical order by the genus name, shown in bold type. On the next line is the most widely used common name. The third line contains the complete botanical name: genus, species, and where applicable, a variety or cultivar name.

Common names vary, but botanical names are the same everywhere. If you learn botanical names, you'll always get the plant you want from a mail-order nursery or local garden center. One gardener's moss pink may be another gardener's mountain pink, but both gardeners will recognize the plant if they know its scientific name: *Phlox subulata*.

When several species in a genus are similar in appearance and cultural needs, they are listed together in a single entry in the chart. In the case of a genus containing two or more vastly different species that cannot be covered in a single entry, each of the recommended species is given a separate entry in the chart.

The second column of the chart provides a brief plant description. Look here to see if the plant is vertical, bushy, low, or creeping. Check here also for flower and leaf descriptions.

▼ Color Range

The color dots following each description indicate the color *family*, and are not a literal rendering of the flower color. A plant given a pink dot might be pale blush pink, clear pink, or bright rose-pink.

▼ Time of Bloom

Blooming time is given by season and varies somewhat from one region of the country to another according to climate, weather, and growing conditions. The Christmas rose, *Helleborus niger*, flowers in January or February in southern gardens, but not until March or April farther north. During a cold year when spring comes late, plants will bloom later.

In warm climates a plant will generally flower in the early part of the range listed; in cooler climates it will usually bloom later. If you want more specific information on when a plant flowers in your area, ask neighbors who grow it or a local garden center or your local USDA county cooperative extension office. As you get to know your garden and its plants, you'll be able to anticipate their flowery display.

▼ Hardiness Zones

Plant hardiness is generally an indication of the coldest temperatures a plant is likely to survive. But many plants also have limits to the amount of heat they can tolerate. In this chart hardiness is expressed as a range from the coolest to the warmest zones where the plant generally thrives. The zones are based on the newest version of the USDA Plant Hardiness Zone Map, shown on page 127.

▼ Growing Conditions

The last column of the chart summarizes the best growing conditions for the plant. Look here for information on the plant's light, moisture, and soil requirements.

		Color Range	Time of Bloom	Growth Habit	Hardiness Zones	Growing Conditions
ACANTHUS ARTIST'S ACANTHUS, BEAR'S-BREECH *Acanthus mollis*	A large plant with 1- to 2-ft. glossy, deep green, spiny leaves and bold 2- to 4-ft. spikes of white or purple-blue tubular flowers. Each flower is surrounded by a spine-tipped, pinkish purple bract. Acanthus *needs plenty of space in the garden.*	○ ●	Mid- to late summer	Height: 2–4' Spacing: 3–4'	6 to 10	Full sun to partial shade. Grows best with some afternoon shade in zones 8–10, requires well-drained soil, and won't tolerate soggy conditions. Mulch during winter north of zone 7. Propagate from seed or divisons of root-stocks.
ACHILLEA YARROW ◀ *Achillea filipendulina* *A. millefolium* *A.* × 'Moonshine' *A. ptarmica*	Excellent border and rock garden plants with flat-topped clusters of white, yellow, or pink flowers, depending upon the species or cultivar. The ferny, gray-green foliage is fragrant when touched. Cut flowers are long lasting.	○ ◕ ○ ●	Late spring to late summer	Height: 1½–3¼' Spacing: 8–12"	3 to 10 A. filipendulina, A. × 'Moonshine' 4 to 8 A. millefolium 3 to 8 A. ptarmica 4 to 10	Full sun to partial shade. Yarrow tolerates hot, dry conditions; too much watering may lead to mildew problems. Many yarrows spread rapidly and should be divided periodically.
ACONITUM MONKSHOOD ◀ *Aconitum napellus* *A. henryi*	Spikes of helmet-shaped, dark blue-violet or white flowers borne on tall stems with decorative dark green, deeply lobed leaves. Monkshood is ideal for a semi-shady border. The roots and other parts of this plant are poisonous.	● ● ●	Midsummer to mid-autumn	Height: 3–5' Spacing: 1–2'	4 to 8	Grows best in cool climates with rich, moist soil and partial shade. Plant grows slowly and is relatively free from pests. Propagate from early-spring or late-fall division or from seed; it takes about 3 years for seedlings to reach flowering size.
ADIANTUM MAIDENHAIR FERN ◀ *Adiantum pedatum* SOUTHERN MAIDENHAIR FERN *A. capillus-veneris*	Some of the most graceful and delicate of the hardy native ferns. The fan-shaped fronds are borne on wiry dark stems arising from rhizomes that spread slowly underground. The spores are clustered on the undersides of the leaflets.	●	Late spring to autumn	Height: 8–18" Spacing: 6–12"	2 to 11 A. pedatum 2 to 8 A. capillus-veneris 9 to 11	Full to partial shade. Grows best in moist, humusy soil. The southern species survives outdoors to zone 7 or 8 or can be grown indoors in colder climates.
ADONIS PHEASANT'S-EYE, AMUR ADONIS *Adonis amurensis*	Bright yellow, buttercup-like flowers about 2 in. across borne on branching stems. Divided, ferny leaves appear after flowers have bloomed and die down in early summer. Pheasant's-eye is often grown in rock gardens.	◔ ○ ●	Early to mid-spring	Height: 8–18" Spacing: 8–12"	3 to 8	Full sun or partial shade and rich soil that is not particularly dry or wet. Propagate pheasant's-eye by seeds or division of dormant roots.

◀ *Indicates species shown*

Perennials for American Gardens

			Color Range	Time of Bloom	Growth Habit	Hardiness Zones	Growing Conditions
	AGAVE CENTURY PLANT *Agave americana*	Primarily a foliage plant, since it takes 10 to 50 years for the dramatic flowering stem to bolt (20–40 ft.) from the rounded mass of thick, spine-tipped, leathery, 5-ft. leaves. It is much smaller when grown indoors in large pots.	● ●	Spring to midsummer	Height: 4–8' Spacing: 4–8'	8 to 10	Full sun and well-drained, sandy-loam soil. The soil should not be allowed to dry out completely during the growing season but should not be wet during the winter. Agave grows outdoors only in relatively frost-free regions.
	AJUGA CARPET BUGLEWEED *Ajuga reptans*	A low, creeping plant that rapidly spreads from stolons. The leaves are dark, glossy green and grow to a height of only 4 in. The spikes of deep blue flowers rise up to 6 in. above the foliage. Cultivars provide color variation in leaves and flowers.	● ● ● ○ ●	Spring to early summer	Height: 6–10" Spacing: 6–18"	4 to 9	Full sun to partial shade with some afternoon shade in warm climates. Soil should not be wet or excessively drained. This ideal ground cover can become weedy if planted with other border or bedding plants.
	ALCHEMILLA LADY'S-MANTLE ◀ *Alchemilla mollis* *A. vulgaris*	A low border and edging plant having particularly attractive, water-repellent gray-green foliage. Tiny yellow-green flowers are borne in loose clusters above the leaves.	● ●	Spring to midsummer	Height: 8–18" Spacing: 1–2'	4 to 8	Full sun to partial shade with ordinary loamy soil and even moisture. Lady's-mantle does not grow well in very wet or very dry soils. It can become somewhat weedy with age and may need to be divided.
	ALOE CANDELABRA ALOE *Aloe arborescens* ◀ *A. brevifolia*	A tall, shrubby plant with thick, gray-green, arching, 2-ft. leaves clumped together in rosettes. The clusters of bright red, tubular flowers are borne on tall, branched stems. A. brevifolia looks like a miniature version and has 3-in. leaves.	● ●	Midwinter	Height: 5–10' Spacing: 1½–2½'	9 to 11	Full sun and well-drained soil. These plants can be grown outdoors only in regions that do not have killing frosts.
	ALSTROE-MERIA LILY-OF-THE-INCAS *Alstroemeria ligtu hybrids*	A clump-forming, bushy plant bearing 6-petaled, 2-in. flowers. Colors are deep red to orange to yellow to pink and streaked or speckled regardless of color. Plants have 6–7 branches of flowering stems, each with several flowers.	● ● ● ● ○ ●	Summer	Height: 1–2' Spacing: 1–2'	7 to 11	Full sun to light shade with constantly moist soil rich in organic matter. Alstroemerias are not hardy in northern climates, but their tuberous roots can be planted out in the spring, dug up in autumn, and stored at 40°F over winter.

			Color Range	Time of Bloom	Growth Habit	Hardiness Zones	Growing Conditions
	AMSONIA BLUESTAR, WILLOW AMSONIA *Amsonia tabernae-montana*	Dense clusters of light blue, 1/2-in. trumpet-shaped flowers that flare out to 5 long-pointed petals. Flowers are borne atop somewhat shrubby stems arising in clumps. The willowlike leaves turn golden yellow in autumn.	●	Mid-spring to early summer	Height: 1 1/2–3' Spacing: 2–3'	3 to 9	Shade to partial sun. Bluestars are easy to grow, but the soil should not be allowed to dry out. Trim back to 12 in. after flowering, unless you want to use pods in flower arrangements.
	ANAPHALIS EVERLASTING, PEARLY EVERLASTING *Anaphalis margaritacea* ◄ *A. triplinervis*	Dense clusters of creamy white, 1/4-in. globular flowers on erect, woolly stems. As the common names imply, these silver-leaved members of the aster family make excellent dried flowers. *A. triplinervis is smaller.*	○	Late summer to autumn	Height: 6–30" Spacing: 6–12"	3 to 9 *A. margaritacea* 3 to 8 *A. triplinervis* 4 to 9	Full sun to very light shade with well-drained, nutrient-poor, dry soil. A. triplinervis is not as drought-tolerant and may need periodic watering in dry spells. Everlastings overwinter best where soils are not wet.
	ANCHUSA BUGLOSS *Anchusa azurea*	Tall plants with hairy stems and leaves. Bugloss has clusters of large, 3/4-in., bright blue flowers that resemble forget-me-nots with white centers. This is sometimes listed in catalogs as A. italica, Italian bugloss.	●	Late spring to early summer	Height: 4–6' Spacing: 1–2'	3 to 8	Full sun to partial shade in well-drained, rich soil. Plants tend to be short-lived, but usually self-sow. Mature plants should be divided every few years to keep them growing vigorously. Prolong flowering by dead-heading fading clusters.
	ANEMONE JAPANESE ANEMONE *Anemone hupehensis* ◄ *A. × hybrida*	Five-petaled flowers borne on thin stems having large, toothed leaves at their bases. Colors range from white to pink to red, all with yellow centers. The dwarf A. hupehensis is smaller than the hybrids (sometimes listed as A. japonica).	○ ● ● ● ●	Late summer to mid-autumn	Height: 1 1/2–4' Spacing: 1–2'	5 to 9 *A. × hybrida* 6 to 8	Full sun to partial shade in humus-rich, well-drained (moist but not wet) soil. Mulch during winter in zones 6 and colder.
	ANTHEMIS ST. JOHN'S CHAMOMILE *Anthemis sancti-johannis* GOLDEN MARGUERITE ◄ *A. tinctoria*	Yellow or orange, 1 1/2- to 2-in., daisylike flowers on branching stems with divided, aromatic, feathery leaves. Deep-orange St. John's chamomile blooms later in the season and is hardy to zone 5.	● ● ●	Mid-spring to mid-autumn	Height: 2–3' Spacing: 1–1 1/2'	3 to 9 *A. sancti-johannis* 4 to 9 *A. tinctoria* 3 to 8	Full sun and ordinary garden conditions or even poor, dry sites. Do not overwater. Anthemis is an excellent cutting flower; cutting extends flowering season. It may become weedy; if needed, rejuvenate mature plants by springtime division.

◄ *Indicates species shown*

Perennials for American Gardens

		Color Range	Time of Bloom	Growth Habit	Hardiness Zones	Growing Conditions
AQUILEGIA ROCKY MOUNTAIN COLUMBINE *Aquilegia caerulea* GARDEN COLUMBINE ◄ *A. × hybrida* *A. vulgaris*	Flowers bearing 5 tubular petals ending in spurs. Petals either match or contrast the brightly colored sepals and golden yellow stamens at the center. Attractive, blue-green leaves have rounded sub-divisions.		Spring to early summer	Height: 2–3' Spacing: 9–18"	3 to 9 *A. caerulea* 3 to 7 *A. × hybrida,* *A. vulgaris* 4 to 9	Full sun to partial shade in humus-rich, well-drained soil. Hybrid columbines tend to be short-lived and should be divided every few years. Remove leaves showing leaf-miner tunnels or stems showing borer damage.
ARABIS WALL ROCK CRESS *Arabis caucasica*	A rapidly growing evergreen ground cover with small clusters of white or pink, cross-shaped flowers rising above a dense mass of gray-green foliage. Arabis looks wonderful cascading over rocks or low stone walls.		Early to mid-spring	Height: 5–10" Spacing: 6–12"	4 to 7	Full sun to partial shade in well-drained to dry soil. Arabis is an easy plant to grow in borders and rock gardens. Divide plants in the early spring if overly mature plants show reduced flowering.
ARENARIA MOSS SANDWORT *Arenaria verna 'Aurea'*	Low, alpine cushion plant with small, white flowers that look like 5-pointed stars. Sandworts are easily grown in rock gardens and even as a ground cover. Flowers are borne on thin stems that emerge from a low mat of dense foliage.		Spring	Height: 2–4" Spacing: 3–6"	3 to 8	Full sun to light shade in well-drained, sandy to loamy soil. Should be lightly mulched during winter in zones 5 and colder. A. verna 'Aurea' is a vigorous grower that can be aggressive.
ARMERIA THRIFT, SEA PINK *Armeria maritima*	A low, mounding plant with grasslike, evergreen leaves. Long stems bear pink flower clusters. White or red forms are also available. Each 1-in.-diameter spherical head has many small, 5-petaled flowers.		Late spring to midsummer	Height: 6–15" Spacing: 6–12"	4 to 8	Full sun and sandy to loamy soil that is well-drained but not excessively dry. A native of coastal Europe, thrift is ideal for seaside gardens but is equally at home in rock gardens, beds, and borders. Divide clumps every several years.
ARTEMISIA WORMWOOD *Artemisia ludoviciana* 'Silver King' *A. schmidtiana* 'Silver Mound'	Mounds of divided leaves covered with soft, silky hairs, giving the foliage a silver-green or woolly, white appearance. The lacy leaves are somewhat fragrant and persist until frost. Flowers are small and gray-white.		Summer to autumn	Height: 1–3' Spacing: 1–2'	4 to 8 *A. ludoviciana* 'Silver King' 5 to 8	Full sun to partial shade and poor, dry soil. Prune occasionally to keep plants growing vigorously. A. schmidtiana is smaller and has darker, finer foliage.

			Color Range	Time of Bloom	Growth Habit	Hardiness Zones	Growing Conditions
	ARUM ITALIAN ARUM *Arum italicum*	A low-growing, spreading plant having spear-shaped leaves with green-yellow veins. The flowers, usually light green or violet, have a leafy bract surrounding a column of tiny flowers. Produces bright red, 1/4-in. berries in summer.		Early spring	Height: 1 1/2–2' Spacing: 6–12"	6 to 11	Full sun to partial shade. Soil should be well-drained, rich in humus, and moist throughout the growing season. Arum can be grown in containers in cold climates. Grows from tuberous root system.
	ARUNCUS GOATSBEARD *Aruncus dioicus*	Looks like a large version of astilbe. Goatsbeard has separate male and female plants, both with sprays of many small, creamy white flowers. The large, compound leaves have toothed edges. Over time plants form large clumps.		Late spring to early summer	Height: 3–6' Spacing: 3–5'	3 to 7	Full sun to partial shade in moist, well-drained, loamy soil. If overmature plants show lack of vigor or flowering, divide the woody rootstocks only while dormant in the early spring.
	ASARUM EUROPEAN WILD GINGER *Asarum europaeum*	Grown as a ground cover where winters are not severe. Glossy, evergreen, heart-shaped leaves arch over to hide three-part, 1/2-in., thimble-shaped, maroon flowers. Rootstocks smell and taste like ginger.		Spring	Height: 6–9" Spacing: 6–12"	5 to 9	Full to partial shade. Wild ginger likes moist, loamy soil that never completely dries out. It is easy to grow and will spread with time. Creeping rootstocks can be easily divided.
	ASCLEPIAS BUTTERFLY WEED *Asclepias tuberosa*	A spectacular native that brings butterflies into the garden. Clusters of ornate flowers range in color from yellow-orange to orange to nearly red. Produces attractive thin pods with plumed seeds in late summer.		Midsummer to late summer	Height: 1 1/2–2 1/2' Spacing: 6–12"	3 to 9	Full sun in well-drained soil. Asclepias does not grow or overwinter well in wet or clayey soil. Seedlings may need watering, but once established, they are very drought resistant. Don't disturb the large tuberous rhizome; propagate from seed.
	ASTER ASTER ◀ *Aster* × *frikartii* 'Wonder of Staffa' *A.* × *frikartii* 'Mönch'	Fragrant, 2- to 3-in., long-lasting, daisylike flowers with bright gold centers. 'Wonder of Staffa' has lavender-blue ray flowers; 'Mönch' has darker blue ray flowers and blooms later in the season.		Midsummer to autumn	Height: 1 1/2–2 1/2' Spacing: 1–1 1/2'	5 to 8	Full sun to partial shade in well-drained but moist soil. Asters are prone to rotting where soils are wet over the winter. Mulch during winter in cooler climates. Divide every several years to keep growth vigorous.

◀ Indicates species shown

Perennials for American Gardens

			Color Range	Time of Bloom	Growth Habit	Hardiness Zones	Growing Conditions
ASTER NEW ENGLAND ASTER *Aster novae-angliae* NEW YORK ASTER *A. novi-belgii*	Tall, hardy natives whose 1- to 2-in. flowers have bright gold centers. Wild forms have purple (N.E. aster) or lavender-blue (N.Y. aster) flowers, but cultivars ranging from white to red to pink are available. Flowers of N.Y. aster are smaller than those of N.E. aster.			Late summer to late autumn	Height: 1–6' Spacing: 1–3'	3 to 8 *A. novae-angliae* 3 to 7 *A. novi-belgii* 4 to 8	Full sun to light shade. Asters like moist soil that is rich in organic matter. Leaves are somewhat susceptible to powdery mildew. Divide mature clumps every 3–4 years to maintain plant's vigor.
ASTILBE ASTILBE *Astilbe × arendsii*	Plumed sprays top stems with deep green, dissected leaves. Astilbes are often hybridized, with many culti-vars available, ranging in color from purple to red to pink to white.			Mid-spring to early summer	Height: 1½–3¼' Spacing: 1–2'	4 to 8	Filtered sun to partial shade with afternoon shade in warm climates. Astilbes need moist, humus-rich soil. Damp, streamside locations are ideal, but avoid water-logged conditions. Astilbes are heavy feeders; fertilize or dress with compost in spring.
ASTRANTIA MASTERWORT *Astrantia major*	Branching flower stems bearing several clusters of tiny, pinkish flowers sur-rounded by long, showy bracts. The deeply lobed leaves grow mostly at the base of the flower stem.			Midsummer	Height: 1½–3' Spacing: 6–12"	4 to 7	Filtered sun to partial shade in moist, humus-rich soil. Damp, streamside locations are ideal; plant will tolerate continually wet soils. Divide mature clumps if they become too large.
AUBRIETA AUBRIETA, ROCKCRESS *Aubrieta deltoidea*	A mat-forming rock garden plant with bright pink, ¾-in. flowers whose 4 petals form a cross. At peak flowering, the soft foliage is hidden below a mass of color. Cultivars with yellow, purple, or blue flowers are available.			Early spring to early summer	Height: 6–9" Spacing: 6–12"	4 to 8	Full sun to partial shade. Plant in well-drained soil or crevices of rocks and walls. Aubrietas are prone to rot if soil is too wet. Prune after flowering to prolong bloom season.
AURINIA BASKET-OF-GOLD, GOLDENTUFT *Aurinia saxatilis*	Upright, yellow clusters held well above small silvery green leaves. As the names imply, this plant bears a pro-fusion of small golden flowers. It is an ideal rock garden plant.			Early to mid-spring	Height: 6–12" Spacing: 6–12"	3 to 9	Full sun to partial shade in well-drained soil. Aurinia tol-erates a wide range of condi-tions. It grows more com-pactly in dry sites than moist ones. Deadhead old flowers to prolong the flowering season.

			Color Range	Time of Bloom	Growth Habit	Hardiness Zones	Growing Conditions
	BAPTISIA BLUE FALSE INDIGO *Baptisia australis*	Indigo blue, pealike, 1-in. flowers borne on long spikes at ends of stout branches. Dark legume pods persist into winter. The foliage is gray-green. Baptisia is slow-growing, but eventually may become large and shrublike.	● ●	Late spring to midsummer	Height: 2–5' Spacing: 2–4'	3 to 8	Full sun to light shade. Baptisia *requires well-drained soil and will not tolerate soggy conditions. It does best in slightly acidic soils.*
	BELAMCANDA BLACKBERRY LILY *Belamcanda chinensis*	Orange flowers mottled with red and borne above 10-in. sword-shaped leaves. Common name derives from the 1/4-in. glossy black seeds that are revealed as the pod ruptures at maturity.	● ● ●	Midsummer to late summer	Height: 2–4' Spacing: 1–1 1/2'	5 to 11	Full sun to light shade in well-drained soil. Blackberry lilies are easy to grow. Mulch during winter in regions colder than zone 7.
	BERGENIA HEART-LEAVED BERGENIA *Bergenia cordifolia*	Heart-shaped, fleshy leaves in dense rosettes. In the early spring, thick stems bearing loose clusters of nodding pink (or white or red) flowers emerge. The foliage turns from lush green to bronze in the autumn.	● ●	Late winter to early spring	Height: 1–1 1/4' Spacing: 6–12"	3 to 9	Full sun to partial shade. Bergenia *grows best with some afternoon shade in warm climates. It prefers well-drained but moist soil. Mulch during winter in zones 3–6.*
	BOLTONIA BOLTONIA *Boltonia asteroides* 'Pink Beauty'	An easy-to-grow native with masses of 1-in. asterlike white flowers with yellow centers. 'Pink Beauty' is one of several cultivars; it has delicate pink flowers. The linear leaves are an attractive gray-green.	○ ● ● ●	Late summer to late autumn	Height: 4–6' Spacing: 3–5'	3 to 9	Full sun to partial shade in well-drained soil that is moist throughout the growing season. Divide the clumps to keep plants from getting too large and too leggy.
	BRUNNERA SIBERIAN BUGLOSS *Brunnera macrophylla*	Attractive, 8-in. heart-shaped leaves. Sprays of 1/4-in., sky blue flowers that resemble forget-me-not rise above the leaves and add further to the effectiveness of this plant in shady borders.	● ●	Early spring to mid-spring	Height: 1–1 1/2' Spacing: 6–12"	3 to 8	Filtered sun to full shade. Brunnera *grows best with some afternoon shade in warm climates but tolerates full sun in cool climates. It prefers well-drained soil that is evenly moist throughout the growing season. Mulch during winter in zones 3-6.*

◀ *Indicates species shown*

Perennials for American Gardens

		Color Range	Time of Bloom	Growth Habit	Hardiness Zones	Growing Conditions
CALTHA MARSH MARIGOLD *Caltha palustris*	Rich yellow, 5-petaled flowers like 1-in. buttercups. Flowers are borne just above bright green, rounded leaves. By early summer (after flowering), plants die back to their underground rhizomes.	●	Spring	Height: 1–2' Spacing: 1–1½'	2 to 8	Full sun to partial shade and soggy, constantly moist soil conditions. Marsh marigold spreads slowly from self-seeding. It is ideal for wetland, streamside, or bog gardens.
CAMPANULA CARPATHIAN HAREBELL *Campanula carpatica* PEACH-LEAVED BELLFLOWER *C. persicifolia*	Blue or white 2- to 3-in. flowers with 5 petals fused into a bell. Shorter (1-ft.) Carpathian harebell has smaller leaves and is more compact than expansive peach-leaved bellflower.	● ● ○ ●	Late spring to midsummer	Height: 8–30" Spacing: 6–18"	3 to 9 *C. carpatica* 3 to 7 *C. persicifolia* 4 to 9	Full sun to light shade. Harebell prefers well-drained, moist garden soil rich in organic matter. Mulch during winter in zones 3–6. Peach-leaved bellflower should be divided in the spring every few years.
CENTAUREA KNAPWEED, PERSIAN CORNFLOWER *Centaurea dealbata*	Bright magenta, 2- to 3-in. flowers with nearly white centers. Leaves are finely divided, bright green above with silvery hairs on their undersides.	● ● ○	Late spring to midsummer	Height: 1½–2½' Spacing: 12–18"	3 to 8	Full sun and well-drained soil. Centaurea will not tolerate soggy conditions. Deadhead fading flowers to promote further flowering. Divide clumps every few years to maintain vigorous condition in plants.
CENTAUREA MOUNTAIN BLUET *Centaurea montana*	Shaggy, 2- to 3-in. flowers, usually cobalt blue, but also available in white, yellow, pink, and purple. The broad leaves are hairy, especially on the underside. Centaurea is an excellent cut flower.	● ● ● ○ ●	Late spring to early summer	Height: 12–18" Spacing: 1–1¼'	3 to 8	Full sun and average, well-drained soil. Mulch during winter in cold climates. Centaurea is an easily grown plant that may become weedy with time. Pruning after the first flowering usually stimulates a second bloom.
CENTRANTHUS RED VALERIAN, JUPITER'S BEARD *Centranthus ruber*	Fragrant, crimson ½-in. flowers borne in dense clusters atop branched, smooth, leafy stems. Cultivars with white or deep red flowers are also available. The clasping leaves are gray-green.	● ● ○	Late spring to midsummer	Height: 2–3' Spacing: 1–1½'	4 to 8	Full sun and well-drained soil. Centranthus is easily grown and ideal for rock gardens, although it can become weedy where soil moisture is abundant. It should be mulched during winter in zones 4–6.

			Color Range	Time of Bloom	Growth Habit	Hardiness Zones	Growing Conditions

CERASTIUM
SNOW-IN-SUMMER
Cerastium tomentosum

Short, branched stems bearing masses of small, tubular white flowers and mats of silvery white, woolly leaves. Flowers emerge in early summer. Deeply notched petals make the flowers resemble large chickweed flowers.

○ Early summer to midsummer Height: 4–10" Spacing: 6–12" 2 to 7 Full sun and well-drained, sandy-loam soil. Prone to rotting in wet soils. Excellent for rock gardens and steep banks, Cerastium spreads quickly and may overrun other, more delicate, plants.

CERATO-STIGMA
LEADWORT
Ceratostigma plumbaginoides

Somewhat zig-zag stems with clusters of 1-in., intense cobalt blue flowers at their tips. Quick spreading, leadwort can be used as a long-stemmed ground cover. Dark green, leathery leaves turn bronze late in the season.

● Midsummer to mid-autumn Height: 12–18" Spacing: 12–18" 5 to 9 Full sun to light shade. Leadwort prefers well-drained soil and does not grow well if soil is too moist. Mulch during winter in zones 5–7.

CHELONE
PINK TURTLEHEAD
Chelone lyonii

A southeastern native that can be grown even in zone 3. The puffy, pink snapdragon-like flowers resemble the heads of turtles. Pairs of dark green, lance-shaped leaves are scattered along the stout stems and provide good contrast to the flowers.

● Late summer to mid-autumn Height: 1–3' Spacing: 8–18" 3 to 8 Full sun to partial shade. Chelone grows best in moist, humus-rich soils; it tolerates soggy conditions and is an excellent choice for a wetland garden.

CHRYSO-GONUM
GREEN-AND-GOLD,
GOLDEN STAR
Chrysogonum virginianum

Single, bright gold composite flowers with pointed petals borne on short stems above a spreading, dense mat of lustrous green leaves. This long-blooming native makes an excellent ground cover or bedding plant.

● Early spring to midsummer Height: 4–8" Spacing: 6–12" 4 to 8 Full sun to medium shade with some afternoon shade in very warm climates. Chrysogonum requires well-drained but moist soil. Mulch very lightly during winter in cooler climates. Remove mulch early in the spring; plants may rot if mulch is too thick.

CIMICIFUGA
BLACK SNAKEROOT
Cimicifuga racemosa
KAMCHATKA BUGBANE
◀ *C. simplex* 'White Pearl'

Bold woodland plants with wands of small (1/2 in.), creamy white, ill-scented flowers borne atop long stems. The large, compound leaves are deeply lobed. C. simplex is smaller and flowers later than the native C. racemosa.

○
○ Midsummer to early autumn Height: 3–8' Spacing: 1–1 1/2' 3 to 8
C. simplex 'White Pearl' 4 to 8 Full sun to partial shade with some afternoon shade in warm climates. Cimicifuga grows best in moist, well-drained soil that is rich in organic matter and not too acidic. Plants grow slowly.

◀ *Indicates species shown*

Perennials for American Gardens

		Color Range	Time of Bloom	Growth Habit	Hardiness Zones	Growing Conditions
COREOPSIS BIGFLOWER COREOPSIS *Coreopsis grandiflora* THREADLEAF COREOPSIS ◄ *C. verticillata* 'Moonbeam'	Bright yellow ray flowers atop masses of spreading greenery. C. grandiflora has 2- to 3-in. flowers and broad, lance-shaped leaves; C. verticillata 'Moonbeam' has thin, wiry leaves, 1- to 2-in. soft yellow flowers, and a mounded growth form.		Late spring to late summer	Height: 1–3' Spacing: 9–12"	3 to 9 *C. grandiflora* 4 to 9	Full sun and well-drained but moist soil. Deadhead fading flowers to prolong bloom. Coreopsis is easy to grow, although C. grandiflora is short-lived. Divide every few years to keep plants vigorous.
CORYDALIS YELLOW CORYDALIS *Corydalis lutea*	Clusters of bright yellow, ³/₄-in. ornate flowers borne on smooth stems above soft, gray-green, fernlike foliage, Corydalis is a perfect plant for shady rock gardens or moist walls.		Mid-spring to midsummer	Height: 8–15" Spacing: 6–12"	5 to 7	Full sun to light shade with some afternoon shade in warm climates. Corydalis grows best in moist, well-drained soils that are rich in organic matter. Corydalis is a self-sower and is sometimes treated as an annual in cooler zones 3–5.
DELPHINIUM CANDLE LARKSPUR *Delphinium elatum*	Tall, stately plants with full spikes of showy blue or purple, 5-sepaled, 4-petaled, 1-in. flowers with light centers. The large, dark green leaves are deeply dissected. Many hybrids of D. elatum have a variety of flower sizes, colors, and shapes.		Late spring to midsummer	Height: 4–6' Spacing: 12"	3 to 7	Full sun and well-drained, moist soil rich in organic matter. Delphiniums are very cold hardy, but do not tolerate droughts or hot nights. Sturdy stems benefit from staking, particularly where it is windy or rainy. Slugs and mildew can cause problems.
DENDRA- THEMA HARDY MUM, FLORISTS' CHRYSAN- THEMUM *Dendrathema × grandi- florum* 'Yellow Spoon'	Available in thousands of cultivars with flower colors ranging from whites, yellows, reds, pinks, lavenders, to tans. Flower shapes vary considerably as do sizes (1–6 in.). Hardy mums are also sold as Chrysanthem × mori- folium.		Late summer through autumn	Height: 1¹/₂–5' Spacing: 1–2¹/₂'	4 to 9	Full sun to light shade. Requires well-drained soil, preferably rich in humus. Pruning the stems in spring will encourage a compact plant form. Mulch during winter in cooler climates. Divide clumps every year or so to keep plants vigorous.
DIANTHUS ALLWOOD PINK *Dianthus × alwoodii* COTTAGE PINK, GRASS PINK ◄ *D. plumarius*	Dense tufts of narrow, grass-like, gray-green leaves, from which emerge stems bearing clusters of 2-in., fragrant, pink (or white, purple, or peach) flowers with 5 petals, usually fringed. Grass pink forms matted cushions and has blue-green foliage.		Early to mid-summer	Height: 6–18" Spacing: 9–15"	3 to 9	Full sun to light shade. Dianthus prefers some after-noon shade in warm climates. Soil should be well-drained and neutral to alkaline. Dianthus needs good air circulation to prevent rusts and fungus. Divide clumps every few years to promote growth.

			Color Range	Time of Bloom	Growth Habit	Hardiness Zones	Growing Conditions
	DIANTHUS SWEET WILLIAM *Dianthus barbatus*	A short-lived perennial sometimes grown as a biennial. The bicolored, 1-in. flowers are often combinations of white, pink, red, salmon, or purple. Dianthus is also available in double-flowered cultivars resembling miniature carnations.	● ● ○ ●	Late spring to midsummer	Height: 5–18" Spacing: 6–12"	4 to 9	Full sun to partial shade. Dianthus *prefers well-drained, neutral to alkaline soil and good air circulation. To avoid fungal problems, do not mulch* Dianthus *during winter. Divide every year to encourage vigorous growth, or grow as a biennial.*
	DICENTRA WILD BLEEDING-HEART *Dicentra eximia* WESTERN BLEEDING-HEART *D. formosa*	Mounds of fernlike, deep-cut leaves. Bears solid rose-pink, 3/4-in. flowers resembling elongated hearts. Long flowering season. Both are natives, but D. formosa *is preferred for the West Coast and D. eximia for the East.*	● ●	Late spring to fall	Height: 1–1½' Spacing: 6–12"	3 to 9 *D. eximia* 3 to 8 *D. formosa* 4 to 9	Full sun to full shade with some afternoon shade in warm climates. Dicentra requires well-drained, moist soil. Mulch during winter in cooler climates. Dicentra may need to be divided if it spreads too rapidly.
	DICENTRA COMMON BLEEDING-HEART *Dicentra spectabilis*	Classic border perennial with foot-long sprays of pendant, pink and white, 1-in., heart-shaped flowers. Lush, gray-green, dissected leaves die back in midsummer. A pure white color form, 'Alba', is available.	● ○	Late spring to midsummer	Height: 1½–3' Spacing: 1½–2½'	3 to 9	Partial sun to partial shade or full sun if soil is sufficiently moist and climate cool. Avoid hot, dry sites. Soil should be well-drained, evenly moist, and rich in humus. Dicentra *tends to be short-lived in zones 8 and warmer.*
	DICTAMNUS GAS PLANT *Dictamnus albus* 'Rubra'	Shrubby perennial with a pungent, lemon-oil scent in its 5-petaled flowers, stems, and glossy, leathery leaves. The 1-in., white or light pink flowers have 10 showy, curved stamens. Cultivar 'Rubra' has lavender-pink petals with dark veining.	● ○ ●	Late spring to early summer	Height: 1–4' Spacing: 3–4'	3 to 8	Full sun to partial shade. Gas plant needs well-drained soils; wet soils may lead to root rot. Propagate from seeds. It does not transplant or divide well, but once established, it is long-lived and easy to care for. May become shrubby with age.
	DIGITALIS FOXGLOVE *Digitalis purpurea*	A biennial that may appear to be a perennial because it self-seeds so freely. Rosettes of thick, soft leaves appear the first year. Second-year flower stalks bear many pink or white tubular flowers, each decorated with contrasting dots.	○ ● ●	Late spring to midsummer	Height: 2–5' Spacing: 10–12"	4 to 8	Full sun to partial shade. Foxglove prefers well-drained soil that is constantly moist. Few pests bother the leaves, the source of the drug digitalis. A vigorous self-seeder, transplant seedlings in fall or early spring.

◄ *Indicates species shown*

Perennials for American Gardens

		Color Range	Time of Bloom	Growth Habit	Hardiness Zones	Growing Conditions
DODECA-THEON SHOOTING-STAR ◄ *Dodecatheon meadia,* *D. clevelandii*	Clusters of small cyclamen-like flowers with 5 reflexed petals. The hardier D. meadia, an eastern native, is usually white but sometimes pink; the western D. clevelandii *is rose. The plant dies back to its rootstock in summer.*	○ ●	Spring	Height: 8–18" Spacing: 12"	3 to 11 *D. meadia* 3 to 8 *D. clevelandii* 8 to 11	Full sun to shade. Soil should be rich in organic matter and moist during the plant's growing season. When dormant, plants can tolerate drier soils.
DORONICUM LEOPARD'S-BANE *Doronicum cordatum,* ◄ *D. pardalianches*	Bright yellow, daisylike flowers excellent for cutting. Heart-shaped leaves clasp the erect stems but may wither under hot, dry conditions. D. pardalianches *is considerably larger than D. cordatum.*	●	Spring	Height: 10–48" Spacing: 1–2'	3 to 8	Full sun to partial shade. Leopard's-bane needs some afternoon shade in warm climates and full sun in cool climates. It grows best in well-drained soil that is both moist and rich in organic matter. Plant in a well ventilated site to prevent mildew.
ECHINACEA PURPLE CONEFLOWER *Echinacea purpurea*	Large daisylike blooms with dusky pink outer petals and a domed, spiny center of iridescent golden bronze florets. Coneflower has coarse, lance-shaped leaves and sturdy flower stems. It is an excellent cut flower.	● ● ● ●	Late spring to autumn	Height: 2–4' Spacing: 1–2'	3 to 8	Full sun to light shade. Coneflower prefers well-drained sandy-loam soil. Relatively drought tolerant and very easy to care for. Makes an ideal meadow plant.
ECHINOPS GLOBE THISTLE *Echinops ritro*	Spherical, 2-in. heads of gray-blue flowers borne on long, branched stems. Like most thistles, Echinops has large, spiny leaves and prickly bases on the flower heads. Flowers last much of the summer.	● ●	Summer	Height: 3–5' Spacing: 1–1½'	3 to 8	Full sun and well-drained soil; these conditions necessary if Echinops is to overwinter in cold climates. Globe thistles will not tolerate soggy conditions and may need staking.
ECHIUM VIPER'S BUGLOSS ◄ *Echium fastuosum* *E. vulgare*	A large, shrubby plant with deeply veined, white woolly leaves. Deep blue ½-in. flowers with long, red stamens are borne in cylindrical clusters of a hundred or so at the tips of the branches. Flower buds look like small pink stars.	● ● ●	Midspring to late spring	Height: 4–6' Spacing: 2–3"	9 to 11 *E. fastuosum* 9 to11	Full sun and well-drained soil. An effective plant for hillside planting in warm climates, bugloss is very fast growing and easy to care for. E. vulgare *is a biennial or a short-lived perennial.*

			Color Range	Time of Bloom	Growth Habit	Hardiness Zones	Growing Conditions
	EPIMEDIUM BISHOP'S-HAT, LONGSPUR EPIMEDIUM *Epimedium grandiflorum*	A very durable ground cover with ornate, long-spurred, 1- to 2-in. flowers of white, red, or violet. The lush foliage is divided into groups of 6 to 9 heart-shaped leaflets. Foliage remains green for most of the year.	● ○ ● ●	Late spring	Height: 8–12" Spacing: 6–12"	4 to 8	Partial to full shade. Epimedium *prefers well-drained, humus-rich soil. Once established, it will tolerate dry conditions. Avoid soggy soils.*
	EREMURUS DESERT-CANDLE ◀ *Eremurus elwesii 'Albus'* *E. himalaicus*	Stems bearing a 2-ft. spike of tiny pink or white flowers with yellow stamens rising from a cluster of 3-ft., fleshy leaves. Flowering progresses from the bottom to the top of the spike. E. himalaicus *is smaller.*	● ● ○	Late spring to midsummer	Height: 3–9' Spacing: 2–4'	5 to 8	Full sun and well-drained soil. Mulch during winter in cooler climates.
	ERIGERON FLEABANE *Erigeron × hybridus*	Leafy stems bearing single, asterlike, 2-in. flowers in pink, light blue, or lavender with yellow centers. These versatile perennials have a relatively long flowering season.	● ● ● ●	Late spring to late summer	Height: 1–1½' Spacing: 6–12"	3 to 8	Full sun to light shade. Fleabane is not at all particular about soil conditions. It is prone to mildew in damp sites with poor ventilation.
	ERYNGIUM SEA HOLLY *Eryngium maritimum*	Thistlelike plant with attractive, blue-gray, spiny foliage and tight, globular heads of small, white to pale blue flowers. Flower heads are surrounded by prickly, leafy bracts.	○ ● ●	Late spring to late summer	Height: 1–1½' Spacing: 6–12"	6 to 8	Full sun and well-drained, sandy soil. As its name suggests, it makes an excellent plant for seaside gardens.
	EUPATORIUM MIST FLOWER, BLUE BONESET *Eupatorium coelestinum*	Flat, ½- to 1-in. clusters of small, ragged, light blue flowers similar to a large ageratum. This perennial flowers from late summer until frost. The 3-in. leaves are triangular and coarsely toothed.	● ● ●	Late summer to autumn	Height: 1½–3' Spacing: 6–12"	6 to 11	Full sun to light shade in well-drained soil. Eupatorium is easy to grow and may become weedy.

◀ *Indicates species shown*

Perennials for American Gardens

	Color Range	Time of Bloom	Growth Habit	Hardiness Zones	Growing Conditions
EUPHORBIA SPURGE ◂ *Euphorbia characias* var. *Wulfenii* CUSHION SPURGE *E. epithymoides* *Insignificant flowers rising from showy, yellow or purple bracts. E. epithymoides forms cushions that turn reddish in autumn; E. characias is more erect and has thicker stems.*		Mid-spring to early summer	Height: 1–3' Spacing: 1½–2'	4 to 11 *E. characias* var. *Wulfenii* 7 to 11 *E. epithymoides* 4 to 9	Full sun to very light shade. Spurges prefer well-drained soil. E. epithymoides grows over a wide range of zones. E. characias var. Wulfenii grows only in southern zones.
FILIPENDULA QUEEN-OF-THE-PRAIRIE *Filipendula rubra* *Beautiful, foamy clusters of tiny, light pink, 5-petaled flowers borne on long stems that also bear bold, deeply lobed, angular leaves. Cultivars with deep red flowers are available.*		Early to mid-summer	Height: 4–6' Spacing: 1–2'	3 to 9	Full sun to light shade. Filipendula prefers well-drained but evenly moist soils rich in organic matter but will thrive even in wet soils. This native is ideal for wet meadows and prairies.
GAILLARDIA BLANKET FLOWER *Gaillardia × grandiflora* 'Goblin' *Showy, daisylike flowers borne on wiry stems above lobed, hairy foliage. A hybrid of native perennial and annual gaillardias, 'Goblin' has bright scarlet, daisylike flowers with yellow, toothed tips. Excellent for borders or even meadows.*		Summer	Height: 1½–2½' Spacing: 1–1½'	4 to 9	Full sun and well-drained soil. In wet soil the plant becomes leggy and is prone to rotting during the winter. Do not fertilize; it does best on nutrient-poor soil with little organic matter. Short-lived, sometimes lasting only two years.
GALIUM SWEET WOODRUFF *Galium odoratum* *An easy-to-grow ground cover that also can be used to flavor wine. The 1- to 2-in. leaves are arranged in whorls of 6–8 around the square stems. The cross-shaped, ¼-in., white flowers are borne in loose clusters above the foliage.*		Spring	Height: 8–12" Spacing: 6–12"	4 to 8	Partial shade and well-drained but evenly moist soils. Galium may spread too rapidly and become weedy in sites with abundant organic matter and moisture.
GAZANIA GAZANIA *Gazania splendens* ·*G. linearis* TREASURE FLOWER ◂ *G. rigens* *Bright, 2- to 3-in. daisylike flowers whose petals have striking color combinations (usually oranges, yellows, browns, and white). Foliage is linear or dissected, gray-green leaves that are woolly white beneath, in rosettes or trailing mats.*		Late spring to early summer	Height: 6–10" Spacing: 6–12"	8 to 11	Full sun. Gazania requires well-drained soil and will not tolerate soggy conditions. Grow as an annual in colder regions.

		Color Range	Time of Bloom	Growth Habit	Hardiness Zones	Growing Conditions
GENTIANA STEMLESS GENTIAN ◀ *Gentiana acaulis* WILLOW GENTIAN *G. asclepiadea*	*Longtime favorites for their intense blue, 1- to 2-in. tubular flowers. G. acaulis only grows about 4 in. high. G. asclepiadea has foot-long arching stems and willowlike leaves and blooms later in the season.*	● ●	*Summer to autumn*	Height: 4–18" Spacing: 4–12"	4 to 8 *G. acaulis* 4 to 7 *G. asclepiadea* 5 to 8	*Full sun to partial shade. Gentian needs some after-noon shade in warm cli-mates. It prefers well-drained soil that is slightly acidic, evenly moist, and rich in organic matter.*
GENTIANA CLOSED GENTIAN, BOTTLE GENTIAN *Gentiana andrewsii*	*Unusual, deep blue flowers borne in whorled clusters near tips of branched stems. The flowers appear to be continually in bud and are pollinated by bees that force their way through the small opening at the tip.*	● ● ●	*Late summer to autumn*	Height: 1–3' Spacing: 1–2'	3 to 8	*Full sun to partial shade. Bottle gentian needs moist soil for best growth. This native thrives where soils are soggy and is an ideal plant for wetland, streamside, or wet meadow planting.*
GERANIUM BLOOD-RED CRANESBILL ◀ *Geranium sanguineum* LILAC CRANESBILL *G. himalayense,* *G. ×* 'Johnson's Blue'	*An informal, spreading plant with showy, 5-petaled flowers borne above mounds of 5-lobed, dissected, deep green leaves. G. sanguineum has rose pink, magenta, or white flowers while 'Johnson's Blue' has violet-blue flowers.*	● ● ○	*Late spring to early fall*	Height: 8–18" Spacing: 1–1½'	3 to 8 *G. sanguineum, G. ×* 'Johnson's Blue' 4 to 8	*Full sun to partial shade with some afternoon shade in warm climates. Cranesbill prefers well-drained soils that are moist and rich in organic matter.*
GEUM AVENS *Geum quellyon*	*Loose clusters of flowers borne on thin stems that arch above mounds of divided, fuzzy, evergreen foliage. The 1½-in., 5-petaled flowers are bright scarlet, orange, or yellow depending upon the cultivar.*	● ● ● ○	*Late spring to midsummer*	Height: 1¼–2' Spacing: 6–12"	4 to 7	*Full sun to partial shade. Geum requires well-drained soil and will not tolerate soggy conditions, especially over the winter. Mulch during winter in cooler climates.*
GYPSOPHILA BABY'S-BREATH *Gypsophila paniculata*	*Informal, airy plants with masses of feathery, ¼-in. white, pink, or reddish flowers borne on wiry stems with pairs of blue-green leaves. Gypsophila makes an excellent dried flower.*	○ ◐ ●	*Summer*	Height: 6–30" Spacing: 1–1½'	3 to 9	*Full sun. Gypsophila prefers well-drained, evenly moist soil that is neutral to slightly alkaline and rich in organic matter. Baby's-breath responds well to the addi-tion of ground limestone. Stake plants as blooms mature.*

◀ *Indicates species shown*

Perennials for American Gardens

		Color Range	Time of Bloom	Growth Habit	Hardiness Zones	Growing Conditions
HELENIUM SNEEZEWEED *Helenium autumnale*	Showy, yellow, daisylike flowers with broad, round-toothed petals and domed centers borne on branched stems that appear winged from extensions of the leaf bases. Cultivars have red, orange, or brown colors in addition to yellow.		Late summer to autumn	Height: 3–5' Spacing: 1–2'	3 to 8	Full sun to light shade with moist soil that is not too clayey. Divide older plants to keep them growing vigorously. May require staking.
HELIANTHE-MUM SUN ROSE, ROCK ROSE *Helianthemum nummularium*	Shrubby, low, spreading evergreen plant with pairs of narrow leaves and clear yellow, pink, or orange 5-petaled flowers on slender stems. Rock rose will cascade over low walls and walkways; it is an attractive edging plant.		Early summer	Height: 8–12" Spacing: 6–12"	6 to 8	Full sun. Rock rose requires well-drained limy soil and will not tolerate soggy conditions. Prune back after flowering to stimulate new, vigorous growth. Mulch during winter in cooler climates.
HELICHRYSUM LICORICE PLANT *Helichrysum petiolatum*	A sprawling, nearly shrubby plant grown for its woolly, heart-shaped leaves. This tender perennial has small (1/4-in.) ivory and yellow flower heads surrounded by creamy white bracts.		Spring to summer	Height: 2–3' Spacing: 1–2'	9 to 10	Full sun and well-drained soil. Licorice plant is good for sandy soils but will spread with age and may need to be trimmed to keep tidy. It can be grown in pots or hanging baskets and moved indoors for winter in colder climates.
HELLEBORUS CHRISTMAS ROSE *Helleborus niger* LENTEN ROSE *H. orientalis*	Deeply divided, glossy evergreen leaves and single, waxy, 1- to 1 1/2-in. flowers borne on sturdy stems. Early blooming H. niger has pink or white flowers; spring-blooming H. orientalis has pink to purple flowers.		Late autumn to late spring	Height: 1–1 1/2' Spacing: 6–12"	4 to 9 H. niger 4 to 8 H. orientalis 5 to 9	Full sun in the winter garden, but at least partial shade in the summer. Hellebores require well-drained, evenly moist soil and benefit from addition of humus and limestone. Mildew and slugs can be a problem. Mulch during winter in cooler climates.
HEMERO-CALLIS DAYLILY *Hemerocallis hybrida* *H. lilioasphodelus*	Plants composed of mounds of grasslike leaves and colorful trumpet-shaped flowers borne on sturdy, erect stems. H. lilioasphodelus is yellow. Many hybrids and cultivars give a staggering array of colors.		Late spring to summer	Height: 1–5' Spacing: 1 1/2–2'	3 to 9	Full sun to light shade with some afternoon shade in warm climates. Daylilies grow best in soil that is rich in organic matter. Roots and rootstocks enlarge with age and need to be divided periodically.

			Color Range	Time of Bloom	Growth Habit	Hardiness Zones	Growing Conditions
	HEUCHERA CORALBELLS ◄ *Heuchera sanguinea* ALUMROOT *H. × brizoides* *H. 'Palace Purple'*	An evergreen plant composed of mounded mats of glossy, round-lobed leaves. Clusters of small, cup-shaped pink, red, or white flowers are borne on leafless, wandlike stems. 'Palace Purple' has deep purple-bronze leaves.	● ○ ●	Late spring to late summer	Height: 1–2' Spacing: 1–1½'	3 to 8 *H. × brizoides, H. 'Palace Purple'* 4 to 8	Partial shade to full sun. Heuchera requires well-drained, humus-rich soil with plenty of moisture; it tends to rot under soggy conditions. These natives are ideal for rock gardens.
	HIBISCUS ROSE MALLOW *Hibiscus moscheutos*	A large plant bearing 6- to 8-in. hollyhock-like flowers with darker "eyes" and a column of creamy white stamens and pistils at their centers. This perennial, native to North American coastal marshlands, assumes shrub-like dimensions.	● ◐ ○	Summer to early autumn	Height: 4–8' Spacing: 3–4'	5 to 11	Full sun and well-drained soil with plenty of organic matter and moisture. Japanese beetles, slugs, and fungal rusts may be a problem. Mulch during winter in zones cooler than zone 7.
	HOSTA PLANTAIN LILY *Hosta fortunei* ◄ *H. sieboldiana* FRAGRANT PLANTAIN LILY *H. plataginea*	A longtime favorite shade-garden plant with attractive lance-shaped leaves in various shades of green (or variegated) with spikes of pastel lavender, blue, or white flowers. Species, hybrids, and cultivars vary in size, shape, and flower color.	◐ ○ ◐ ○	Early summer to fall	Height: 1–3' Spacing: 1–2'	3 to 8	Low-maintenance plants that grow well in shade, partial shade, or even full sun if the soil is sufficiently moist. Hostas are prone to rotting if the soil is not well-drained. Slugs and deer may eat leaves. Mulch during winter in cooler climates.
	IBERIS EVERGREEN CANDY-TUFT *Iberis sempervirens*	Clusters of showy, yet small, bright white flowers borne on nearly obscure mats of 1½-in., narrow, deep green leaves. Iberis is an ideal plant for rock gardens or hanging baskets.	○	Early to mid-spring	Height: 6–12" Spacing: 1–1½'	3 to 9	Full sun to very light shade. Iberis prefers well-drained, humus-rich soil. Prune after flowering to promote reblooming and more vigorous growth. Mulch during winter in cooler climates.
	INCARVILLEA HARDY GLOXINIA *Incarvillea delavayi*	Trumpet-shaped, 2- to 3-in. yellow to rosy purple tubular flowers with 5 rounded lobes borne in clusters on 1- to 2-ft. stems above mounds of 10-in. fernlike leaves. Foliage resembles leaves of Jacob's Ladder (Polemonium).	● ◐	Late spring to early summer	Height: 1–2' Spacing: 1–1½'	5 to 8	Sunny but protected locations or partial shade with well-drained soil. Hardy gloxinia does not thrive under hot, dry conditions. Mulch during winter in cooler climates.

◄ *Indicates species shown*

Perennials for American Gardens

			Color Range	Time of Bloom	Growth Habit	Hardiness Zones	Growing Conditions
	INULA INULA *Inula ensifolia*	Single, 1½-in. flowers resembling bright yellow, thin-petaled daisies with darker yellow centers borne on smooth stems. Narrow, pointed leaves. Plants form clumps over time.	● ●	Midsummer	Height: 1–1½' Spacing: 6–12"	3 to 9	Full sun to light shade. Inula prefers well-drained but moist soil. Plants are prone to mildew. Provide good air circulation to minimize this tendency.
	IRIS SIBERIAN IRIS *Iris sibirica*	Delicate, 2-to 3-in. blue, purple, yellow, or white flowers borne on erect, sturdy stems that rise amidst long, saberlike leaves. Plants grow in compact clumps. Many cultivars are available in varying colors and sizes.	● ● ○	Late spring to midsummer	Height: 1–3' Spacing: 1–2'	3 to 8	Full sun to partial shade. Siberian iris thrives in normal, well-drained, moist garden soil. Irises are easy to grow.
	IRIS BEARDED IRIS *Iris × germanica*	Sturdy plants with fanned displays of broad, swordlike leaves that rise from thick rhizomes just at the soil surface. Tall stems bear several large flowers with 3 broad, upright petals and 3 wide, bearded sepals. Available in many colors.	● ● ● ● ● ○ ●	Late spring to midsummer	Height: 1–4' Spacing: 1–2'	3 to 9	Full sun to partial shade. Bearded iris prefers well-drained soil rich in organic matter. Divide every 3–5 years to keep plants growing and flowering vigorously. Remove withering foliage to reduce borer problems.
	KNIPHOFIA TORCH LILY, RED-HOT POKER *Kniphofia uvaria*	A spectacular plant for temperate regions. A floral shaft bearing a cylindrical cluster of small tubular flowers rises above tufts of narrow, bright, evergreen leaves. The flower cluster is bright red at the tip and yellow at the base.	●	Late spring to summer	Height: 3–5' Spacing: 1–2'	5 to 9	Full sun and average well-drained soil that is evenly moist, at least while the plant is becoming established. Kniphofia is drought tolerant once established, but prone to rotting if soil is too wet. Mulch during winter in cooler climates.
	LAMIUM SPOTTED DEAD NETTLE ◄ *Lamium maculatum* WHITE DEAD NETTLE *L. album*	Creeping perennials with 1- to 2-in., lustrous, attractively variegated leaves and clusters of rosy pink, 1-in., double-lipped flowers. L. album *has white flowers.*	● ● ○	Late spring to summer	Height: 6–12" Spacing: 6–8"	4 to 9	Dappled sun to partial shade and well-drained, moist soil. With time the plant spreads, making it an attractive ground cover or a bit of a weed.

			Color Range	Time of Bloom	Growth Habit	Hardiness Zones	Growing Conditions
	LATHYRUS PERENNIAL PEA *Lathyrus latifolius*	A climbing vine that bears clusters of 1- to 2-in. pealike flowers in white, pink, red, or lavender. The flowers lack the fragrance of sweet peas, but the plant grows more vigorously.	○ ● ● ●	Midsummer to early autumn	Height: 4–8' Spacing: 1½–2½'	4 to 9	Full sun and well-drained, moist soil. Support this climber with a stone wall, fence, or trellis. Remove withering blossoms to promote further flowering. Lathyrus *is prone to mildew and rotting if soil is too wet.*
	LEUCAN-THEMUM SHASTA DAISY *Leucanthemum × superbum*	Daisylike 3-in. flowers with pure white outer petals and bright yellow centers borne singly on sturdy stems. Cultivars with double or all-yellow flowers are available. Shasta daisy is often listed as Chrysanthemum × superbum.	○	Late spring to midsummer	Height: 1–3' Spacing: 9–15"	3 to 11	Full sun to light shade. Shasta daisy prefers well-drained, evenly moist soil. Remove faded blossoms to extend the flowering season. Plants are easy to grow.
	LIATRIS SPIKE GAY-FEATHER *Liatris spicata* 'Kobold'	Small, rosy lavender, shaggy flowers massed on a floral shaft that blooms from the top toward the bottom of 1- to 2-ft. stems. The lower halves of the stems are covered with attractive, grasslike leaves.	● ● ●	Midsummer to early autumn	Height: 1–5' Spacing: 6–12"	3 to 9	Full sun and well-drained but moist soil that is rich in organic matter. Divide clumps of stems if flowering decreases with time. Liatris is easy to grow.
	LIGULARIA BIGLEAF LIGULARIA *Ligularia dentata*	A bold perennial with 5-in. yellow-orange, gold, or orange daisylike flowers borne in flat, branched clusters on sturdy stems. Large (1- to 2-ft.) kidney-shaped, toothed, bright green leaves form large masses.	● ● ●	Mid- to late summer	Height: 3–4' Spacing: 2–3'	3 to 8	Light to partial shade. Ligularia needs well-drained soil with plentiful moisture. It is susceptible to slugs and snails. Ligularia is an ideal poolside plant, but requires much room. Mulch during winter in cooler climates.
	LINARIA TOADFLAX *Linaria genistifolia*	Erect, graceful plants bearing delicate, snapdragon-like 1- to 2-in. bright yellow flowers with orange throats and a long spur projecting backward from the flower's lower lip. The stems have clasping, 1¼-in.-long leaves.	● ●	Late spring to midsummer	Height: 1½–2½' Spacing: 6–12"	4 to 8	Full sun to partial shade in well-drained, normal garden soil. Toadflax is much better behaved in the garden than butter-and-eggs, its weedy relative.

◄ *Indicates species shown*

Perennials for American Gardens

		Color Range	Time of Bloom	Growth Habit	Hardiness Zones	Growing Conditions
LOBELIA CARDINAL FLOWER *Lobelia cardinalis*	A moisture-loving plant with erect spikes of scarlet flowers crowning leafy stalks. The brilliant red flowers resemble small flying birds and attract hummingbirds and butterflies alike. Ideal for streamside and wetland gardens.	● .	Midsummer to midautumn	Height: 1–5' Spacing: 6–12"	4 to 9	Full sun to partial shade. Lobelia *grows best in organic-rich soils with constant moisture; it also grows in average, evenly moist garden soil. Mulch during winter in cold climates where frost heaving may present a problem.*
LUPINUS LUPINE *Lupinus polyphyllus*	Pagoda spires of pealike flowers in blues, yellows, reds, white, or combinations rising from compound leaves. Russell hybrids (a cross between L. polyphyllus *and other lupine species) offer the widest choices in color and size.*	○ ● ● ● ● ● ●	Late spring to midsummer	Height: 3–5' Spacing: 1–2'	3 to 7	Full sun to partial shade. Lupines need some afternoon shade to protect them from the heat in warm climates. They prefer well-drained soil that is rich in organic matter, slightly acidic, and evenly moist.
LYCHNIS MALTESE-CROSS ◀ *Lychnis chalcedonica* ROSE CAMPION, MULLEIN PINK *L. coronaria*	Brilliant scarlet, 5-petaled flowers clustered on tall stems with pairs of clasping, oval leaves. Spring-blooming rose campion has similar, but deep rose-pink, flowers and silver foliage. The stems of both quickly form clumps.	● ●	Spring to mid-summer	Height: 2–3' Spacing: 1–1¼'	3 to 9 *L. chalcedonica* 4 to 8	Full sun to light shade and well-drained, humusy, evenly moist soil. Divide every few years to maintain plant vigor. Rose campion may be short-lived, but reseeds freely.
LYSIMACHIA GOOSENECK LOOSE-STRIFE *Lysimachia clethroides* GARDEN LOOSESTRIFE ◀ *L. vulgaris*	Erect plants with arching stems bearing hairy, lance-shaped leaves and crowned with groups of star-shaped flowers. L. clethroides has clear white flowers on a drooping stem, while L. vulgaris has bright yellow flowers on an erect stem.	○	Late spring to midsummer	Height: 1–3' Spacing: 9–15"	4 to 8	Full sun to partial shade and evenly moist, well-drained soil rich in organic matter. Loosestrifes need moisture and cannot withstand prolonged drought. They spread vigorously and need frequent division to keep them in check.
MACLEAYA PLUME POPPY *Macleaya cordata*	Small, creamy white or pinkish flowers arranged in plumes on tall, leafy stems. Large (8- to 10-in.), gray-green leaves are fuzzy white beneath and deeply lobed. Plants become rather shrubby after a few years.	○ ●	Late spring to late summer	Height: 6–10' Spacing: 2–3'	3 to 9	Full sun to partial shade. This rapid grower is not at all fussy about soil conditions and can be invasive. Plant it where it can have plenty of space and keep an eye on it. Remove suckers to keep it under control.

			Color Range	Time of Bloom	Growth Habit	Hardiness Zones	Growing Conditions

MALVA
HOLLYHOCK MALLOW
Malva alcea

Erect, shrubby plants bearing hollyhock-like 2-in. flowers in white, pink, or rose. A short column bearing the stamens and pistils rises from the centers of the flowers. Leaves are deeply lobed and covered with short hairs.

Early summer to midsummer

Height: 2–3'

Spacing: 6–12"

4 to 8

Full sun to partial shade. Malva grows best in well-drained, ordinary garden soil. Easily propagated by division.

MERTENSIA
VIRGINIA BLUEBELLS
Mertensia virginica

A strikingly beautiful native of moist deciduous wood-lands. Sprays of delicate flowers are pink in bud, powder blue in full flower, and fade to pink with age. By midsummer the entire top of the plant dies back and disappears.

Midspring to late spring

Height: 1–2'

Spacing: 1–1¼'

3 to 8

Full sun to partial shade. Mertensia needs well-drained soil rich in organic matter and moist throughout the growing season. It will not tolerate dry conditions and may be troubled by slugs and snails.

MONARDA
BEEBALM,
OSWEGO TEA
Monarda didyma

Bright, round clusters of red, 2-lipped, tubular flowers borne on slender, square stems. Flower heads are sur-rounded by colored, leafy bracts. Cultivars come in pink, lavender, and white.

Early summer to late summer

Height: 2–3'

Spacing: 6–12"

6 to 8

Full sun to partial shade. Monarda prefers well-drained, moist, humus-rich soil. It tolerates very wet soil but is prone to mildew if allowed to become too crowded. Divide periodically to maintain vigor and keep in check.

MYOSOTIS
FORGET-ME-NOT
◄ *Myosotis alpestris*
M. scorpioides

Early spring, mat-forming plants bearing coiled clusters of clear blue, 5-petaled flowers with yellow or white centers. The flowers of M. alpestris are quite fragrant.

Spring to mid-summer

Height: 3–6"

M. alpestris 5 to 7

Spacing: 6–12"

3 to 11

Dappled sun to partial shade with some afternoon shade and additional moisture in warm climates. Forget-me-not prefers well-drained, evenly moist soil and does not tolerate drought very well. It may become weedy.

NEPETA
CATMINT,
CATNIP
Nepeta × faassenii
'Six Hills Giant'

A plant grown as much for its showy clusters of ½-in. blue or lavender flowers as for its aromatic, gray-green foliage. 'Six Hills Giant' has deep purple flowers. Forms mounds with age.

Late spring to midsummer

Height: 2–3'

Spacing: 1–1¼'

3 to 8

Full sun to partial shade. Well-drained, average garden soil works well. Prune back after flowering to maintain vigorous condition and encourage a second blooming.

◄ *Indicates species shown*

Perennials for American Gardens

		Color Range	Time of Bloom	Growth Habit	Hardiness Zones	Growing Conditions
OENOTHERA SHOWY PRIMROSE *Oenothera speciosa*	Large (3-in.) flowers with 4 broad, pink or white petals and a yellow, cross-shaped stigma borne on thin, creeping stems. After a day, the flowers turn deeper pink.	●○	Late summer to early autumn	Height: 1½–2' Spacing: 6–12"	5 to 9	Full sun to partial shade. Evening primrose is drought tolerant and grows best in well-drained soil. This native may become invasive over time but is easily pulled.
OPUNTIA PRICKLY PEAR CACTUS *Opuntia humifusa* ◀ *O. engelmannii*	A cactus with oval pads studded with prominent, stiff spines. O. humifusa, with showy, yellow blossoms, grows best in the eastern U.S.; O. Engelmannii, bearing yellow, orange, or red flowers and edible burgundy fruit, is a southwestern desert native.	○	Late spring to early summer	Height: 10–15" Spacing: 1–1½'	4 to 11 O. humifusa 4 to 10 O. engelmannii 8 to 11	Full sun and well-drained soil are essential. Opuntia will not tolerate soggy conditions. Mulch during winter in cooler climates, but don't let the pads rot. It may spread rapidly in sandy soil in warm climates.
OSMUNDA CINNAMON FERN *Osmunda cinnamomea*	An attractive, compact, mid-sized fern with sterile green fronds that grow around cinnamon-brown fertile fronds at the center of the clump. Fronds are twice-cut with rounded leaflet lobes.	●	Spring to early autumn	Height: 1½–2½' Spacing: 1–1½'	3 to 8	Full sun to partial shade. Osmunda grows best in damp to wet soils that are acidic and rich in organic matter.
PAEONIA CHINESE PEONY *Paeonia lactiflora* PEONY ◀ *P. officinalis*	Longtime favorite plants with large, saucer-shaped flowers crowning arched stems with lush, lance-shaped leaves. Peonies come in many colors, from white to pink to red to orange to yellow, with single or double sets of petals.	○○●●●	Spring to early summer	Height: 1½–2' Spacing: 1–2'	2 to 8 P. officinalis 4 to 8	Full sun to partial shade. Peonies need well-drained, humus-rich, evenly moist soil and will not tolerate soggy conditions. They may be troubled by slugs and snails. Mulch during winter in cold climates to protect from frost heaving.
PAPAVER ORIENTAL POPPY *Papaver orientale*	Cup-shaped, 3- to 4-in. flowers with 4 broad, crepe-like petals borne on stout stems above lobed, hairy foliage. A ring of dusky stamens surrounds the center flower. Traditional forms are orange, but cultivars are available in red, white, salmon, or pink.	●●●●○	Late spring to early summer	Height: 2–3' Spacing: 1–1½'	2 to 7	Full sun to partial shade. Poppies prefer well-drained, humus-rich soil. They tend to die back to the roots after flowering. Mulch during winter in cooler climates, but remove mulch very early in the spring.

			Color Range	Time of Bloom	Growth Habit	Hardiness Zones	Growing Conditions
	PENSTEMON BEARD-TONGUE *Penstemon cobaea* *P. grandiflorus* ◄ *P. hybrids*	*Striking native and hybrid plants with erect stems bearing open clusters of showy, tubular, 5-lobed flowers in purple, white, pink, or lavender. P. grandiflorus tends to be taller and bears larger flowers.*	● ● ● ● ○	Late spring to midsummer	Height: 2–4' Spacing: 1–1¼'	4 to 8	Full sun. Penstemon *requires well-drained soil and will not tolerate soggy conditions. Mulch during winter in cooler climates.*
	PEROVSKIA RUSSIAN SAGE *Perovskia atriplicifolia*	*Tall, graceful plants bearing pairs of attractive, grayish, aromatic leaves on square stems. Airy sprays of silvery blue flowers top the shrubby stems.*	● ● ●	Early summer to early autumn	Height: 3–5' Spacing: 1–1½'	4 to 9	Full sun and well-drained, sandy-loam soil. Perovskia *will not tolerate soggy conditions. Mulch during winter in cooler climates.*
	PHLOX PERENNIAL PHLOX *Phlox paniculata*	*Clusters of fragrant, 1-in. flowers crowning erect stems clothed in smooth, lance-shaped leaves. Modern cultivars and hybrids have added bright reds, pinks, oranges, purples, and bicolors to the old-fashioned white or lavender palette.*	○ ● ● ● ● ● ●	Midsummer to early autumn	Height: 2–4' Spacing: 1–1½'	4 to 8	Full sun to partial shade and well-drained, evenly moist soil. Phlox *is prone to mildew where humidity and temperatures are high, but this rarely kills the plant. Plant where air circulation is good.*
	PHORMIUM NEW ZEALAND FLAX *Phormium tenax* 'Tricolor'	*A large plant for warm-climate gardens with plenty of space. Striking, sword-shaped, 5-in.-wide leaves grow up to 9 ft. with red-orange lines on their margins. The dull red flowers grow in clusters above the center of the foliage.*	●	Summer	Height: 8–10' Spacing: 5–10'	9 to 11	Full sun to light shade. This fast-growing plant prefers well-drained soil, but can withstand periodically wet soil or drought. However, it is prone to root rot if soil is wet for prolonged periods.
	PHYSOSTEGIA OBEDIENT PLANT, FALSE DRAGONHEAD *Physostegia virginiana*	*A tall, graceful plant with lance-shaped, toothed leaves clasping square stems that are topped by conical spires of shell-pink, rose, or lavender tubular flowers. White cultivars are also available.*	● ● ● ○	Late summer to early autumn	Height: 2–4' Spacing: 1–1½'	3 to 8	Full sun to partial shade. Physostegia *needs shade in warm climates. It tolerates average soil conditions as well as relatively nutrient-poor or damp soils.*

◄ *Indicates species shown*

Perennials for American Gardens

		Color Range	Time of Bloom	Growth Habit	Hardiness Zones	Growing Conditions
	PLATYCODON BALLOON FLOWER *Platycodon grandiflorus*	● ●	Midsummer	Height: 1–3' Spacing: 1–1¼'	3 to 8	Full sun and well-drained soil with ample moisture throughout the growing season. Mulch during winter in cold climates.
A showy plant with balloon-shaped flower buds that open into 3-in. blue, cupped flowers with 5 pointed lobes. Varieties and cultivars come with white or pink flowers. As flowers open, stems need staking.						
	POLEMONIUM JACOB'S-LADDER *Polemonium caeruleum* ◄ *P. foliosissimum*	● ○ ●	Late spring to late summer	Height: 1–2½' Spacing: 8–12"	2 to 7 *P. foliosissimum* 4 to 8	Full sun to partial shade. Jacob's-ladder prefers well-drained soil that is evenly moist and rich in humus. Mulch during winter in cooler climates.
An eastern native with attractive, pinnately divided, ladderlike leaves on the lower halves of long stems that bear loose clusters of bell-shaped blue (or sometimes white), 5-petaled, ½-in. flowers.						
	POLYGO-NATUM SOLOMON'S-SEAL *Polygonatum biflorum*	○	Spring	Height: 1–2½' Spacing: 1–1¼'	3 to 8	Partial sun to full shade. Soil should be rich in organic matter, well-drained, and evenly moist throughout the growing season. Solomon's-seal may be troubled by slugs and snails.
A native eastern woodland plant grown for the visual appeal of its pairs of ⅓-in. blue-black berries as much as the ¾-in. greenish white, tubular flowers that dangle below its arching stems. Solomon's-seal is a good foliage plant.						
	POLYGONUM SNAKEWEED *Polygonum bistorta* 'Superbum'	●	Midsummer to autumn	Height: 1–3' Spacing: 6–12"	3 to 8	Full sun to partial shade. This plant likes moist soils and will not tolerate dry conditions. It may spread extensively with age and need division to keep under control.
A clump-forming plant with lush, 6-in. lance-shaped leaves in a dense mass of foliage below slender stems bearing dense, cylindrical clusters of tiny pink flowers. *Polygonum* is an ideal plant for the streamside or wet garden.						
	POTENTILLA CINQUEFOIL *Potentilla atrosanguinea*, ◄ *P. nepalensis*	● ● ● ●	Summer	Height: 1–2' Spacing: 1–1½'	3 to 8 *P. atrosanguinea* 5 to 8	Full sun to very light shade. Cinquefoil prefers well-drained, sandy-loam soil. Plants tend to form shrubby clumps with age.
A low, spreading plant with compound, strawberry-like leaves and showy 5-petaled, 1-in. flowers. P. atrosanguinea has deep red flowers (some cultivars are salmon) and P. nepalensis has rose-red flowers.						

		Color Range	Time of Bloom	Growth Habit	Hardiness Zones	Growing Conditions
PRIMULA JAPANESE PRIMROSE *Primula japonica* POLYANTHUS PRIMROSE ◄ *P. × polyantha*	Showy, 5-petaled flowers crowning stalks that rise above rosettes of long, spatula-shaped leaves. Primulas come in many different color forms. P. japonica *is taller but has smaller flowers than the P.* polyantha *hybrids.*	● ● ○ ● ● ● ●	Spring to early summer	Height: 1–2' Spacing: 6–12"	3 to 8 P. japonica 6 to 8	*Partial sun to partial shade. Both grow best in well-drained, constantly moist, humus-rich soil. Primulas will not tolerate dry conditions. They may be troubled by slugs and snails. Mulch during winter in cooler climates.*
PULMONARIA LUNGWORT, JERUSALEM SAGE ◄ *Pulmonaria officinalis* BETHLEHEM SAGE *P. saccharata*	An interesting ground cover clothed in attractive, mottled, hairy leaves. Bell-shaped flowers grow above the foliage in linear clusters. P. officinalis *has white or red flowers and P. saccharata has blue flowers that turn pink with age.*	● ○ ● ●	Spring	Height: 8–18" Spacing: 6–12"	3 to 8	*Full to partial shade. Pulmonaria* likes moist, humus-rich soil and does not grow well in dry conditions. It may be troubled by slugs and snails. Periodic division will stimulate vigorous blooming.
RODGERSIA RODGERSIA *Rodgersia pinnata*	An ideal wet or bog garden species with striking pinnately compound leaves. The small flowers, white with red insides, are borne in large, plumed clusters above the dense foliage.	○ ● ●	Late spring to early summer	Height: 3–4' Spacing: 1½–2½'	4 to 7	*Full to partial shade. Rodgersia grows best in well-drained but constantly moist, humus-rich soil. It will not tolerate dry conditions. This plant needs considerable space.*
RUDBECKIA BLACK-EYED SUSAN *Rudbeckia fulgida*	Single, 2-in., daisylike flowers with deep yellow tips and domed, silky, deep brown centers crowning stems with long, lance-shaped leaves. Rudbeckia *is a North American native that is easy to grow almost anywhere.*	● ●	Midsummer to early autumn	Height: 1–3' Spacing: 9–15"	4 to 9	*Full sun to very light shade. Rudbeckia prefers well-drained soil and grows well in average garden soil. A short-lived perennial, it re-seeds well and may become weedy. It is an ideal plant for wildflower meadows.*
SALVIA VIOLET SAGE *Salvia × superba*	Sun-loving, erect plants topped with narrow, dense spikes of tubular, ½-in. purple flowers with 2 prominent lips. Aromatic leaves grow in pairs along square stems. Violet sage spreads slowly to form dense clumps.	● ●	Early to mid-summer	Height: 1–3' Spacing: 1–1½'	4 to 7	*Full sun to light shade. Salvia prefers well-drained but evenly moist soil that is rich in organic matter. Prune after flowering to promote vigorous growth and to prolong blooming. Mulch during winter in cooler climates.*

◄ *Indicates species shown*

Perennials for American Gardens

		Color Range	Time of Bloom	Growth Habit	Hardiness Zones	Growing Conditions
SANTOLINA LAVENDER COTTON *Santolina chamaecyparissus*	A low-growing, aromatic plant useful for edging. Its flowers look like the golden centers of daisies without the white rays. Dense, tiny, woolly gray foliage covers stems and remains year-round.	●	Summer	Height: 1–2' Spacing: 6–12"	6 to 8	Full sun and well-drained sandy-loam soil. Santolina will not tolerate soggy conditions. Mulch during winter in cooler climates.
SAPONARIA ROCK SOAPWORT *Saponaria ocymoides*	A cushion plant with a dense tuft of ¹/₂-in. leaves that are nearly obscured by masses of small (¹/₄ in.), bright pink (or sometimes white), 5-petaled flowers. Saponaria makes an excellent rock garden plant.	● ○	Early summer	Height: 4–8" Spacing: 6"	3 to 7	Full sun to light shade and well-drained soil. Soapwort will not tolerate soggy conditions. Trim back after flowering to maintain compact form.
SAXIFRAGA LONDON PRIDE ◀ *Saxifraga umbrosa* *S. × urbium*	A nice rock garden plant bearing open clusters of small pink or white, 5-petaled flowers on leafless stems. Succulent, toothed, evergreen leaves form a carpet of rosettes.	● ○	Late spring to midsummer	Height: 8–14" Spacing: 6–12"	5 to 8	Dappled sun to full shade. This saxifrage grows best with full shade in warm climates. It requires well-drained, evenly moist soil and will not tolerate soggy conditions. Mulch during winter in cooler climates.
SCABIOSA SCABIOUS, PINCUSHION FLOWER *Scabiosa caucasica*	An old-fashioned perennial with 2- to 3-in. blue (or white), flat flower heads perched on thin, branched stems. Gray-green, divided foliage grows mostly near the base of the stem. Scabiosas are excellent cut flowers.	● ● ● ○	Summer	Height: 1–2' Spacing: 6–12"	3 to 7	Full sun to light shade and well-drained, neutral to slightly alkaline soil that is evenly moist. Scabiosa does not grow well in wet soils. Cutting flowers prolongs the season of bloom.
SEDUM STONECROP ◀ *Sedum sieboldii* × 'Ruby Glow' *S. spectabile* × 'Autumn Joy'	Erect, clump-forming plants bearing thick, succulent leaves, notched or wavy-toothed edges. Small red or pink, 5-petaled flowers are borne in dense clusters above thick, sturdy stems. S. sieboldii tends to be smaller than S. spectabile.	● ● ●	Late summer to mid-autumn	Height: 6–24" Spacing: 6–12"	3 to 9 *S. sieboldii* 'Ruby Glow' 6 to 9	Full sun to partial shade. Sedums prefer well-drained, humus-rich soil, but these drought resistant plants thrive even if neglected.

			Color Range	Time of Bloom	Growth Habit	Hardiness Zones	Growing Conditions
	SIDALCEA CHECKERBLOOM *Sidalcea malviflora*	A Pacific Coast native that bears miniature pink hollyhock-like flowers on slender stems. Rounded, fuzzy leaves have piecrust edges and long stalks. Flowers open with the morning sun and twist closed at night.	● ●	*Late winter to late spring*	Height: 8–30" Spacing: 8–12"	7 to 11	*Full sun to partial shade. Sidalcea prefers well-drained soil that is evenly moist and does not grow well if the soil is dry during the growing season. Prune back after flowering. Mulch during winter in cooler climates.*
	SILENE INDIAN PINK *Silene californica*	A native of the Sierra Nevada and Coastal Range. This low plant has 1- to 1¹⁄₂-in., bright red, 5-petaled flowers. Each petal has several rounded lobes, giving flowers a fringed look. Pairs of 2-in., dark green leaves clasp the stems.	●	*Midspring to midsummer*	Height: 6–18" Spacing: 6–12"	7 to 11	*Partial sun to partial shade. Silene requires well-drained soil and will not tolerate soggy conditions, particularly when it is dormant following flowering. Mulch during winter in cooler climates.*
	SISYRINCHIUM BLUE-EYED GRASS ◄ *Sisyrinchium bellum* *S. angustifolium*	Native plants with grasslike leaves and narrow stems crowned with clusters of 1-in. blue flowers with yellow centers. S. bellum should be grown in California and mild climates, while the eastern S. angustifolium is hardier.	● ● ●	*Early spring to midspring*	Height: 5–15" Spacing: 6–12"	3 to 11 *S. bellum* 9 to 11 *S. angustifolium* 3 to 8	*Full sun to partial shade. S. bellum requires well-drained soil that is moist in the growing season but dry during the dormant season. S. angustifolium is not particular about soils and makes an excellent meadow plant.*
	SMILACINA SOLOMON'S-PLUME, FALSE SOLOMON'S-SEAL *Smilacina racemosa*	A woodland native with a cluster of tiny, white, foamy flowers at the tips of each arching stem and clasping leaves that tend to be purple at their points of attachment. Beautiful red berries appear in summer.	○ ○	*Midspring to early summer*	Height: 1–2¹⁄₂' Spacing: 9–12"	3 to 8	*Dappled sun to full shade. Solomon's-plume grows best with some afternoon shade in warm climates. It prefers well-drained, evenly moist, humus-rich soil. It will grow in full sun, but will be smaller. Mulch during winter in cooler climates.*
	STACHYS LAMB'S-EARS *Stachys byzantina* 'Silver Carpet'	A low, dense ground cover bearing soft, woolly, silver leaves. This slowly creeping plant forms dense clumps with age.	●	*Late spring to midsummer*	Height: 6–18" Spacing: 6–12"	4 to 8	*Full sun to partial shade. Stachys needs well-drained soil and tends to rot under soggy conditions. Mulch during winter in cooler climates.*

◄ *Indicates species shown*

Perennials for American Gardens

		Color Range	Time of Bloom	Growth Habit	Hardiness Zones	Growing Conditions
STOKESIA STOKES' ASTER *Stokesia laevis*	Spectacular, ragged-petaled, clear blue, 2- to 3-in. flower heads with lighter centers borne on branched stems with shiny, deep green leaves. Stokes' aster is an attractive and versatile perennial for beds and borders.	●●◐○	Summer	Height: 1–2' Spacing: 6–12"	5 to 9	Full sun to partial shade. Stokesia prefers well-drained, evenly moist soil; once established, it will tolerate moderately dry conditions. It may be troubled by slugs and snails. Mulch during winter in cooler climates.
TANACETUM PAINTED DAISY, PYRETHRUM *Tanacetum coccineum* 'Roseum'	Bright red 3-in. flowers with yellow centers borne on long, single stems. Pink and rose color forms are also available. The long-lasting blooms make excellent cut flowers. Painted daisy is also sold as Chrysanthemum coccineum or T. collineum.	●●◐	Early to mid-summer	Height: 1½–2' Spacing: 9–12"	5 to 8	Full sun and well-drained, loamy soil. Mulch during winter in cooler climates.
TANACETUM FEVERFEW *Tanacetum parthenium*	Bright green, fragrant, lobed foliage, with abundant, small ³/4-in. daisylike flowers with yellow centers, and many rows of stubby, white ray florets. A medicinal plant in colonial gardens. Also sold as Chrysanthemum parthenium.	○○◐	Midsummer to autumn	Height: 1–3' Spacing: 8–15"	3 to 11	Full sun to light shade and well-drained soil rich in humus. May become weedy through self-seeding if soils are constantly moist. Treat as an annual in zone 3, but provide winter mulch in zones 4–6.
TEUCRIUM GERMANDER *Teucrium chamaedrys* 'Prostratum'	A shrubby, low perennial with dense masses of small (³/4-in.), aromatic leaves. Grown more for its foliage texture than the small spikes of reddish purple, 2-lipped flowers, Teucrium makes a nice edging plant.	●	Late summer	Height: 8–12" Spacing: 6–12"	4 to 11	Full sun. Teucrium grows best in well-drained, sandy-loam soils. It makes an excellent low hedge for warm-climate rock gardens.
THALICTRUM MEADOW RUE *Thalictrum speciosissimum*	A tall plant with bluish gray-green, dissected leaves and loose pyramids of pale yellow, ¹/8-in. flowers crowning tall, stout stems. The handsome foliage is useful in creating flower arrangements.	○	Summer	Height: 2–5' Spacing: 6–12"	5 to 8	Full sun to partial shade. Thalictrum prefers well-drained, moist, humus-rich soil. Mulch during winter in cooler climates.

			Color Range	Time of Bloom	Growth Habit	Hardiness Zones	Growing Conditions
	THERMOPSIS CAROLINA LUPINE *Thermopsis caroliniana*	A handsome native of the pea family with erect, lupinelike clusters of light yellow flowers at the tops of stiff stems. Compound leaves have 3 gray-green leaflets.		Late spring to early summer	Height: 3–5' Spacing: 1–1³/4'	3 to 8	Full sun to partial shade. Thermopsis *prefers well-drained, evenly moist soil to start out. Once established, the deep roots make it quite drought tolerant. Propagate by division since seeds are slow to germinate.*
	TRADES- CANTIA SPIDERWORT *Tradescantia × andersoniana*	A long-blooming plant composed of dense clumps of erect, fleshy stems bearing blue-green grasslike foliage. Flowers last less than a day, but dozens of buds in each cluster give this hybrid of native spiderworts a long blooming season.		Late spring to midsummer	Height: 1–2' Spacing: 12–20"	3 to 9	Full sun to partial shade. Well-drained but moist soil rich in organic matter. Mulch during winter in cooler climates. Divide clumps every few years to keep them flowering vigorously.
	TROLLIUS GLOBEFLOWER *Trollius europaeus*	A moisture-loving plant bearing bright yellow or orange, globular, double flowers above highly dissected, rich green leaves. A long season of bloom makes this attractive for many garden situations.		Late spring to midsummer	Height: 1–2' Spacing: 6–12"	5 to 8	Full sun to partial shade. This plant likes ample moisture and soils that are well-drained and rich in humus. Mulch during winter in cooler climates.
	VALERIANA VALERIAN, GARDEN-HELIOTROPE *Valeriana officinalis*	A scented herb attractive to cats and bearing clusters of creamy white or pinkish ¹/4-in. funnel-shaped flowers atop tall, leafy stems. Leaves are deeply divided.		Late spring to midsummer	Height: 3–5' Spacing: 6–12"	4 to 8	Full sun to light shade. Valerian is easy to grow and not terribly fussy about soil conditions. It spreads rapidly by extending its roots and through self-seeding. Thin periodically to keep it under control.
	VERBASCUM NETTLE-LEAVED MULLEIN *Verbascum chaixii*	A stately plant bearing columns of light yellow, 5-petaled flowers with contrasting purple stamens. Cultivars with white flowers are available. Leaves of all members of this species are gray-green and thick.		Late spring to midsummer	Height: 2–3' Spacing: 9–12"	4 to 8	Full sun and well-drained soil are about the only requirements for this robust perennial. Verbascum often self-sows.

◀ *Indicates species shown*

Perennials for American Gardens

			Color Range	Time of Bloom	Growth Habit	Hardiness Zones	Growing Conditions
	VERBENA VERVAIN *Verbena bonariensis* ◄ *V. rigida*	A creeping, low-growing plant bearing many colorful, globular clusters of small (1/4-in.), 5-petaled flowers. V. bonariensis is erect and has narrow, toothed leaves at the base of square stems. V. rigida is hardier, has larger, purple flowers and a bushier form.	● ● ○	Summer	Height: 1–2' Spacing: 1–1³/₄'	4 to 11 V. bonariensis 7 to 11 V. rigida 4 to 9	Full sun. Verbena prefers well-drained, humus-rich, moist garden soil. Mulch during winter in cooler climates.
	VERONICA SPEEDWELL ◄ *Veronica incana* *V. spicata*	A low, spreading plant bearing lance-shaped gray-green leaves and conical spikes of small, blue, tubular flowers. The shorter V. incana has hairy leaves; V. spicata has white and rose cultivars as well as blue ones.	● ○ ○ ● ○	Late spring to midsummer	Height: 1–1¹/₂' Spacing: 6–12"	3 to 8 V. spicata 4 to 8	Full sun to partial shade. Veronica needs well-drained but moist soil for optimum growth. Mulch during winter in cooler climates.
	VIOLA HORNED VIOLET *Viola cornuta* SWEET VIOLET ◄ *Viola odorata*	Old-fashioned, woodland plants bearing lush, low-growing 1- to 3-in. leaves and colorful, irregular-shaped flowers. V. cornuta has rosettes of evergreen leaves and larger flowers than V. odorata. The flowers of V. odorata are deliciously fragrant.	● ● ● ● ○ ○ ●	Spring	Height: 4–12" Spacing: 6–12"	4 to 9 V. cornuta 5 to 9 V. odorata 4 to 8	Full to partial shade. Violets prefer moist, humus-rich soil. They slowly creep by rhizome growth or self-seeding. Under ideal conditions they may become a bit rampant.
	YUCCA ADAM'S-NEEDLE *Yucca filamentosa*	A southeastern native that forms clumps of tough, spine-tipped, 2-ft., light gray-green leaves. From the center grows a branched flower stalk bearing many waxy, white, 2-in. pendant flowers.	○ ○	Summer	Height: 5–12' Spacing: 3-6'	4 to 9	Full sun to partial shade. Yucca requires well-drained soil; it tolerates drought but not soggy conditions. The plant center dies after flowering, but offshoots continue to flourish. Mulch during winter in cooler climates.
	ZANTE-DESCHIA GARDEN CALLA, ARUM LILY *Zantedeschia aethiopica*	A plant with bold, deep green, 18-in. leaves arising from a rhizome and striking white, funnel-shaped bracts surrounding bright golden yellow spadices. Callas are not really lilies; they are distantly related to Jack-in-the-pulpits.	○ ○ ○	Late spring to midsummer	Height: 2–3' Spacing: 1–1¹/₂'	9 to 11	Full sun to partial shade. This tropical plant likes plenty of moisture and organic matter. While sensitive to hard frosts, it can be grown as a greenhouse plant in almost any climate.

Plant Hardiness Zone Map

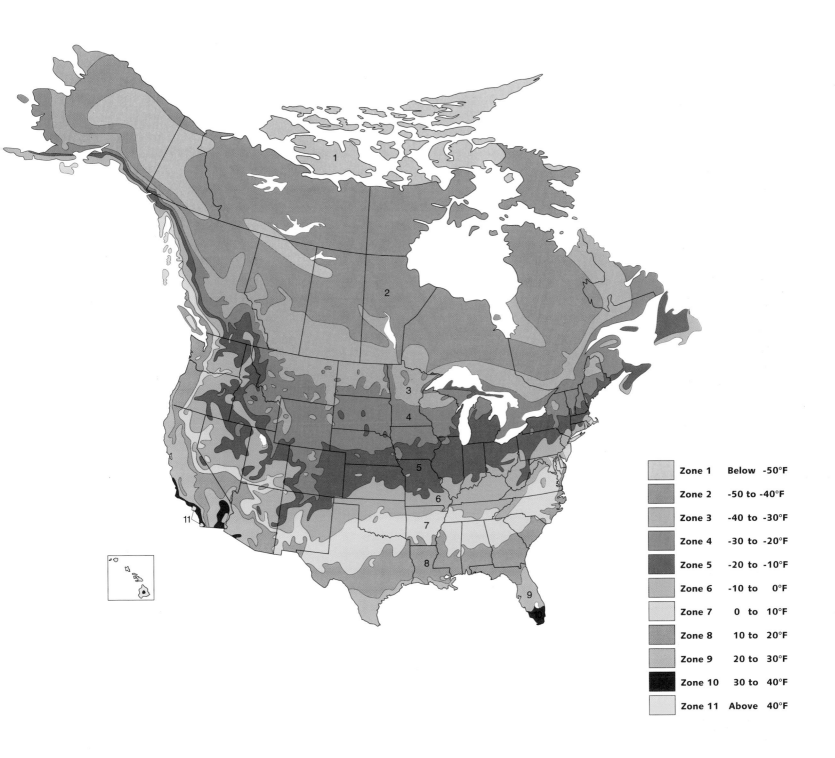

	Zone 1	Below -50°F
	Zone 2	-50 to -40°F
	Zone 3	-40 to -30°F
	Zone 4	-30 to -20°F
	Zone 5	-20 to -10°F
	Zone 6	-10 to 0°F
	Zone 7	0 to 10°F
	Zone 8	10 to 20°F
	Zone 9	20 to 30°F
	Zone 10	30 to 40°F
	Zone 11	Above 40°F

Mail-Order Sources for Perennials

There are many dependable mail-order suppliers that can be helpful for perennial gardeners. A selection is included here. Most have catalogues available upon request (some charge a fee). For further information and supplier suggestions, *The Complete Guide to Gardening by Mail* is available from the Mailorder Association of Nurseries, 8683 Doves Fly Way, Laurel, MD 20723. Please enclose $1.00 for postage and handling in the United States ($1.50 for Canada).

Plants and Seeds

W. Atlee Burpee Co.
300 Park Ave.
Warminster, PA 18991
800-888-1447
Seeds and supplies from one of the oldest names in American gardening.

André Viette Farm and Nursery
Route 1, Box 16
Fishersville, VA 22939
703-943-2315
Over 60 years of growing and selling perennials for sun and shade. Over 3000 varieties.

Bluestone Perennials
7211 Middle Ridge Rd.
Madison, OH 44057
800-852-5243
Sells perennials and selected shrubs, ornamental grasses, and ferns.

Gurney's Seed and Nursery Co.
110 Capital Street
Yankton, SD 57079
605-665-4451
Seeds, plants, and tools for flower and vegetable gardeners.

Holbrook Farm and Nursery
P.O. Box 368
115 Lance Rd.
Fletcher, NC 28732
704-891-7790
Specializes in perennials, wildflowers, and selected trees and shrubs.

Jackson & Perkins
P.O. Box 1028
Medford, OR 97501
800-292-4796
Though known for roses, they also sell perennials, trees, and shrubs, as well as a collection of garden ornaments.

Klehm Nursery
Route 5, Box 197
Penny Rd.
South Barrington, IL 60010
800-553-3715
Grows and sells peonies, daylilies, hostas, grasses, ferns, and many other perennials.

Milaeger's Gardens
4838 Douglas Ave.
Racine, WI 53402-2498
800-669-9956
Over 300 varieties of perennials, including grasses and vines.

Park Seed Co.
Cokesbury Rd.
Greenwood, SC 29647
800-845-3369
Catalogue offering seeds, plants, bulbs, tools, and a wide selection of gardening supplies.

Shady Oaks Nursery
112 10th Ave. S.E.
Waseca, MN 56093
507-835-5033
Good selection of plants that grow well in shade, including hosta, wildflowers, and ferns.

Spring Hill Nurseries
6523 N. Galena Rd.
P. O. Box 1758
Peoria, IL 61656
800-582-8527
Plants and bulbs, specializes in flowers, shrubs, ground covers, and houseplants.

Stokes Seeds, Inc.
Box 548
Buffalo, NY 14240
716-695-6980
Flower and vegetable seeds and supplies for commercial farmers and home gardeners.

Thompson & Morgan
P.O. Box 1308
Jackson, NJ 08527
908-363-2225
Seeds of all types and a wide range of other garden supplies.

Wayside Gardens
1 Garden Lane
Hodges, SC 29695
800-845-1124
Sophisticated ornamental plants, including many hard-to-find perennials.

White Flower Farm
P.O. Box 50
Litchfield, CT 06759
203-496-9600
Shrubs, perennials, supplies, books, gifts. Particularly beautiful color catalogue.

Regional Specialties

Busse Gardens
13579 10th St. N.W.
Cokato, MN 55321
612-286-2654
A wide selection of plants, especially noted for cold-hardy, rare perennials.

Johnny's Selected Seeds
Foss Hill Rd.
Albion, ME 04910
207-437-9294
Particularly useful for cold-climate selections of flowers, herbs, and vegetables, with many fast-maturing, disease-resistant varieties.

High Altitude Gardens
P.O. Box 1048
Hailey, ID 83333
208-788-4363
Seeds and plants that will
thrive in high altitudes.

Kilgore Seeds
1400 W. First St.
Sanford, FL 32771
407-323-6630
Seeds carefully selected
for their ability to grow in
Florida.

Native Seeds/SEARCH
2509 N. Campbell #325
Tucson, AZ 85719
602-327-9123
Native seeds of the
Southwest and Mexico,
collected and propagated
with long-term preserva-
tion in mind.

Niche Gardens
1111 Dawson Rd.
Chapel Hill, NC 27516
919-967-0078
Perennials selected and
propagated for their
ability to survive heat.

Nichols Garden Nursery
1190 N. Pacific Highway
Albany, OR 97321
503-928-9280
Good selection of vari-
eties well-suited for the
Northwest. Many fast-
maturing flowers and
herbs that warm-climate
gardeners can also use.

Porter & Son Seedsmen
P.O. Box 104
Stephenville, TX 76401
Features many older,
hard-to-find varieties.
Also modern hybrids that
resist pests, diseases, and
hot weather.

Redwood City Seed Co.
P.O. Box 361
Redwood City, CA 94064
415-325-7333
Old varieties and a few
new ones, including many
unusual imports.

Supplies and Accessories

Alsto's Handy Helpers
P.O. Box 1267
Galesburg, IL 61401
800-447-0048
Offering classic garden
furniture and accessories,
container plants, and gift
items.

Country Home Products
Ferry Rd., Box 89
Charlotte, VT 05445
802-425-2196
Mowers, trimmers, clip-
pers, composters, and various garden tools.

Garden Way, Inc.
102nd St. & 9th Ave.
Troy, NY 12180
800-833-6990
518-235-6010
Mowers, rototillers,
garden carts, and various

other lawn and garden
equipment.

Gardener's Eden
P.O. Box 7307
San Francisco, CA 94120
800-822-9600
Catalogue offers many
items appropriate for gardeners and some orna-
mental shrubs and
outdoor containers.

Gardener's Supply Co.
128 Intervale Rd.
Burlington, VT 05401
800-955-3370
Useful gardening products
including gifts and accessories, greenhouse kits,
and composters.

Kemp Company
160 Koser Rd.
Lititz, PA 17543
717-626-5600
Shredders, chippers, com-
posters, and supplies.

Kinsman Company
River Rd.
Point Pleasant, PA 18950
800-733-5613
Tools and equipment.
Known for black steel
modular arches that are
easy to assemble and
maintain.

Mantis
1028 Street Rd.
Southampton, PA 18966
800-366-6268
Lawn and garden equip-

ment, including tillers,
chippers, and mowers.

Plow & Hearth
301 Madison Rd.
Orange, VA 22960
800-866-6072
Outdoor furniture and
garden accessories.

Smith & Hawken
2 Arbor Lane
P.O. Box 6900
Florence, KY 41022
800-776-3336
Tools and garden supplies
as well as gardening hats,
shoes, and clothing.

Organic Gardening Products

BioLogic
18056 Springtown Rd.
P.O. Box 177
Willow Hill, PA 17271
717-349-2789
Suppliers of biological
insect-control products.

Gardens Alive!
5100 Schenley Place
Lawrenceburg, IN 47025
812-537-8652
Beneficial insects and a
complete line of supplies
for organic gardening.

Necessary Trading Co.
One Nature's Way
New Castle, VA 24127
703-864-5103
Catalogue includes insec-
ticidal soaps, beneficial
insects, botanicals,

traps, and other natural
products.

Ringer Corporation
9959 Valley View Rd.
Eden Prairie, MN 55344
612-941-4180
Organic soil amendments,
beneficial insects, garden
tools, and irrigation
equipment.

Safer, Inc.
189 Wells Ave.
Newton, MA 02158
617-964-0842
Pest controls, insecticidal
soaps, natural and botan-
ical herbicides.

Erth-Rite, Inc.
RD1, Box 243
Gap, PA 17527
800-332-4171
Organic soil amendments,
Erth-Rite fertilizer, and
other soil enhancers.

Index